"Jim Stump, in *The Power of One-on-One* ity and surprising influence of a persona faith and providing mentorship, it seems, does not require the pomp and circumstance of a vast arena—a cup of coffee and an open ear will do the trick."

—**Pat Williams**, cofounder and senior vice president of the Orlando Magic; author of *Coach Wooden's Greatest Secret*

"I met Jim during my first year of college. He was and is someone I look up to. There is something about his walk with Jesus that is infectious. Joy overflows in his life. He is uniquely wired to connect men twice his size to the Creator and Savior of the world. Jim's discipleship ministry is amazing. He has loved people into a life-changing relationship with his Savior by spending time with them and speaking into their lives in ways that are Spirit-empowered. You will be encouraged and challenged by his story. Perhaps, like me, you will see God calling you to invest more deeply in the lives of others as you read this book."

—**Jay Barnes**, president, Bethel University, St. Paul, Minnesota

"The Bible tells us that a wise man wins souls (Prov. 11:30). Jim Stump is a wise man. He walks the walk of a lifestyle evangelist and has done so for more than thirty years. His platform for sharing hasn't been a street corner or a church building; it has been a table in the athletic dorm of Stanford University. He sets up shop and takes appointments with the athletes to talk with them about the issues of life. He shares the Bible one-on-one as he points these athletes in the right direction for living, and through his work he has led many to a relationship with Christ. No telling how many men he has mentored over the years and how many more he has influenced with his one-on-one mentoring life and message. In this book Jim encourages and inspires all of us to share our faith in a practical, conversational way through imparting the skills and insight he has developed over more than three decades of ministry. I encourage everyone who wants to live wisely to read this book!"

—**Tom Lane**, executive senior pastor, Gateway Church, Southlake, Texas

"Jim Stump has been practicing for years what many desire to do— build disciples one-on-one in small, intimate settings. Learn from the one who mastered Jesus' command to 'go and make disciples.'"

—**Josh D. McDowell**, author and speaker

"Jim Stump lives what he preaches—the power of God to change lives through relationship, one person at a time. I grew up with 'Stumper,' have known him since high school, and this I know: Jim loves God; Jim lets God's love spill over to those around him; Jim listens and laughs and prays, letting the truth about Jesus shine through. Walk with Jim through these pages as he shares what God has taught him about the power of one-on-one mentoring, and discover that God can use you too."

—**Neta Jackson**, author of the Yada Yada Prayer Group series

"One of the primary roles of the Fellowship of Christian Athletes is to reach coaches, who are so much more to athletes than just a person who draws up the plays. The best coaches are great mentors who invest in the lives of their athletes. In *The Power of One-on-One*, Jim Stump shows us why it is so important to be a mentor and how to mentor as Jesus did. *The Power of One-on-One* can be taken to heart as we 'sow into the lives of others in order to reap a harvest of salvation.'"

—**Les Steckel**, veteran NFL coach; president/CEO
of Fellowship of Christian Athletes

"We live in such an age of hyperbole, false advertising, and untruths that it is so refreshing to read of the life of Jim Stump and his mission. Jim does not embellish or try to sell a view of the truth; his book is an authentic extension and explanation of his life. What an inspiring and clear articulation of what it means to follow Jesus and to simply be instructed in the expression of daily walking the talk. *Everyone who is involved in caring for others*, whether in a formal ministry or like most of us attempting to follow Jesus and his teachings, will find not only an interesting story but a life-challenging and helpful expression of the practical living out of one's faith in Jesus. This extends into mentoring and equipping others. We don't need more how-to books and programs; we need more authentic people who model what it means to walk the talk and who express it as Jesus did—nonjudgmentally and in ways that are helpful for equipping the church for the work of ministry. Jim lives out the 'new commandment' in John 13:34–35. Be encouraged by a true follower of Jesus who is faithful to his calling!"

—**Milt Richards**, associate, International Foundation, Pacific Rim

I'm so blessed by your friendship!

Jim

9/24/15

THE
POWER
— OF —
ONE-ON-ONE

THE
POWER
OF
ONE-ON-ONE

Discovering the Joy and Satisfaction of Mentoring Others

JIM STUMP
WITH FRANK MARTIN

BakerBooks

a division of Baker Publishing Group
Grand Rapids, Michigan

Published by Baker Books
a division of Baker Publishing Group
P.O. Box 6287, Grand Rapids, MI 49516-6287
www.bakerbooks.com

Printed in the United States of America

Library of Congress Cataloging-in-Publication Data is on file at the Library of Congress, Washington, DC.

ISBN 978-0-8010-1584-7 (pbk.)

Author is represented by the literary agency of Alive Communications, Inc., 7680 Goddard Street, Suite 200, Colorado Springs, CO 80920, www.alivecommunications.com.

To protect the privacy of those who have shared their stories with the author, some details and names have been changed.

14 15 16 17 18 19 20   7 6 5 4 3 2 1

To my wife, Linda—thank you for loving me
and traveling with me through life.

To my children, Ashley, Mike, and Jason—I am so proud
of who you are becoming as you faithfully continue to
walk with Jesus. Thank you for being willing to adjust
your lives to God's agenda to achieve his purposes.

To my father and mother, Don and Lorene Stump—
thank you for modeling God's love, faithfulness,
and heart for those who have yet to find a relationship with Jesus. Your rewards are many in heaven!

To my siblings, Dave, Don, John, Priscilla Judge,
Mary Lou Elliott, and Zona Wilson—
those sibling reunions are a delicious taste
of what awaits us when we leave this earth.

And finally to Bud Hinkson—it took the uniqueness of who
you were and your amazing vision to attract me to explore
what this journey entailed. And what a journey it has been!
The principles you taught me are being passed on through
generations of men I have mentored. Our loss is heaven's gain!

Contents

Foreword

There is a unique power in a conversation that happens face-to-face, one-on-one, in private moments between two human beings. Many of our defining moments take place in this setting. Marriages get proposed, jobs get offered, counsel is given, confessions are whispered—our secrets get revealed and our life trajectories get altered in the sheltered atmosphere of two friends.

And this is supremely true of the soul. We see this in the life of Jesus all the time. The longest recorded conversation in the New Testament takes place between Jesus and (a big surprise in the ancient world) a Samaritan woman at a well. Jesus goes face-to-face with tax collectors and lepers and prostitutes and fishermen and politicians and, just before he dies, with a thief on the cross next to him.

But this is not just in the Bible. You know it in your own existence, as do I. It has been in the hushed privacy of one-on-one conversations that I have learned many of my deepest lessons about following Jesus. I first learned the power of confession there—the liberation and healing that came the first time I opened up all the secrets and shames of my life to another human being in the presence of Jesus. Some of my most helpful confrontations have happened there—confrontations that I used to dread and yet (while I suppose I do still dread them) have learned to love because of the way they help me grow.

If you were to visit the town of Palo Alto, California, and perhaps wander around the campus of Stanford University, the most likely way that you'd run into Jim Stump would be to see him engaged in an earnest, quiet conversation with somebody over a cup of coffee about those issues in life that matter the most but are least talked about. Jim understands the sheer spiritual power of one life intersecting with another in an intentional, Spirit-filled way.

In a sense, in the chapters that follow, you'll actually get the gift of some one-on-one time with Jim. In this book, the low-key, highly approachable, listen-first style that opens the doors of so many hearts to Jim will become his gift to you. You'll get a sense for what a little creative spirituality can do to bring someone closer to God. I love the story of how Jim challenged a student to play Ping-Pong for some spiritual stakes and then revealed that he hadn't even begun to play with his good hand. Like a scene out of *The Princess Bride*.

But the best part of an encounter like this is the Guest who shows up. Jesus said a long time ago that wherever two or three are gathered in his name, he's right there. Jim has probably pulled together more "gatherings of two" than just about anybody I know. And now the two are Jim and you.

And one more.

John Ortberg
Senior pastor of Menlo Park Presbyterian Church
Author of *Who Is This Man?*

Acknowledgments

In the process of writing a book, there are so many people involved without whom it would have never come to fruition. Words are inadequate to express my thanks for your help in getting this done, but let me start by thanking Rick Christian, the founder of Alive Communications. If you had not picked up that phone and refused to hang up until I agreed to write this book, it may never have happened. Thanks to Tim MacDonald and Al Mueller for encouraging you to call.

Joel Kneedler, thanks for holding my hand and gently leading me through this process, both as my agent and as my new friend. Your relationships and credibility in the publishing industry opened the door to Baker Books when it probably would have been closed in the face of a new, no-name author.

Frank Martin, your gift with words and their proper flow has captured what I want to communicate. I could not have asked for a more professional collaborator for my first book.

Baker Books, you have fulfilled all the great things I heard about you in the publishing world. I am honored that you chose this book out of the many manuscripts that come your way.

Jon Wilcox, thanks to you and your team at Baker Books for taking a chance on a new author who has never done anything but sit at a table hour after hour, meeting with athletes. You are a brave man. You kept the book well structured and did a superb job of editing.

Jeff Barton, you and I both know the role you played so unselfishly, without which this book might not have gotten off the ground in such a timely manner.

John Jenks, your constant encouragement to put down my experiences in book form was instrumental in this book becoming a reality. Thank you for being my mentor and friend.

Dwight Nyquist, you have been a dear friend to me and to the Stump family since I was in high school. You modeled important principles for me regarding how to relate to people and the importance of striving for excellence in everything I do. You have been invaluable to me as a coach, a friend, and a mentor.

Jeff Siemon and Dennis Sheehan, these wonderful four-plus decades began with your invitation to me to come to Stanford. Your credibility opened the doors for me there and laid the foundation for what God has accomplished on the Farm since then.

I have been gifted with wonderful board members who have encouraged me and prayed for me. I could not do this without your leadership. You are a blessing to me!

Andy Chan, thank you for being my "Stanford eyes."

To all those individuals who have invested financially and prayerfully in Sports Challenge—your returns will be bountiful in eternity.

To the scholar-athletes and coaches I have had the joy of mentoring—you have made a huge impact on my life. I cannot thank you adequately for the relationships we enjoy together.

There are others too numerous to mention who have stood by me and encouraged me in so many ways. You know who you are and how much I love and appreciate you!

Note to the Reader

Before we begin our journey together, I want to take a minute to address an issue that is sure to cross your mind as you start to read. You'll notice that many of the stories and anecdotes I've included incorporate only the subject's first name, and a few of the facts surrounding these people may seem vague and incomplete. I've done this intentionally in order to protect the identities of many of the men I've mentored through the years. The stories I've written are real and factual, but a good number of the names and specifics are not.

As a spiritual mentor to a lot of high-profile students and athletes, I have an obligation to my mentorees to keep the things they share with me in the strictest confidence. Mentoring is a sacred trust, and it would be wrong of me to betray that trust for the sake of a book.

If I were to share actual names, you would likely recognize most of the men in these stories, since almost all have gone on to develop high-profile careers in sports, business, politics, or ministry. But that fact makes it even more critical in my eyes to keep their true identities hidden. So if you think you recognize someone from one of my stories, chances are you're wrong.

In some cases, I've used actual names that you're sure to recognize. In those cases, I was given direct permission to share both their names and their stories.

Thanks for understanding, and for taking the time to join me on this exciting journey!

Introduction

One-on-One

One cannot transform a world except as individuals in the world are transformed, and individuals cannot be changed except as they are molded in the hands of the Master.

—Robert Coleman

Back in the late 1990s, I received a call from one of the Stanford Cardinal football recruiters. He told me that a young recruit would be visiting the campus that weekend, and he wanted me to meet him.

As a spiritual mentor, I'm often asked by coaches to speak to their teams or counsel a student who has been struggling with personal issues. This particular recruit was apparently an avid outdoorsman who loved to hunt and fish. Since I had grown up in the wilds of Alaska and used to hunt and fish for a living, the coach thought the two of us would have an immediate bond.

I wasn't naïve. I knew that this coach was more interested in getting this young man to play for Stanford than he was in providing him spiritual counsel, but I never miss an opportunity to meet a new player.

The young man's name was Andrew, and he was an All-American high school player from the Northwest. He was a nationally ranked tight end with a long list of athletic accomplishments, including being named "Best in the West" by the *Long Beach Press*. He had earned nine varsity letters in high school, had excelled at academics, and was a member of the National Honor Society. Almost every major college in the country was courting him, and Stanford was pulling out all the stops to sign him.

I was scheduled to meet him at a reception for potential recruits at one of the nicest hotels in the area. Before walking into the banquet hall, we were all given name tags in the lobby. I entered the room and immediately spotted this enormous, powerfully built young man standing next to the punch table. Our eyes met, and without hesitation he came striding across the room toward me. He looked like a bear that had just spotted supper.

Without introducing himself, he planted himself right in front of me, poking his finger into my chest. "I know who you are," he bellowed, "and I know you play Ping-Pong. I want you to know that I've never been beaten in Ping-Pong, and if I come to Stanford I'm going to kick your butt!"

I took a step back, gathered my composure, and said, "If you decide to come to Stanford, I'd love to take you on in a match."

I've met a lot of competitive athletes in my day, but he was one of a kind.

Earning the Right to Be Heard

The fall season rolled around, and sure enough, Andrew had accepted the scholarship that Stanford offered him. I was on the sidelines during the team's first day of practice, and he was every bit as good as they said he was.

When practice ended, he spotted me on his way to the locker room and immediately headed in my direction. Once again he towered over me, this time his dirt-smeared face dripping sweat. "I want you at the Ping-Pong table tonight at eight o'clock!" he thundered.

I just smiled and nodded.

I was thirty minutes late meeting him at the players' dorm that night, and he had already warmed up by easily beating several of the other students. I stood and watched for a few minutes as he finished a match, and I could see why he was so confident. He was as fast as lightning, with amazing hand-eye coordination.

He dominated the game, winning his last point with a powerful kill shot to the corner of the table, then glared over in my direction. "Okay, Stump," he snarled. "Your turn!"

I shot him a quick grin, shook my head, and said, "No, Andrew, that's not the way it works around here. Here's what's going to happen. If you beat me, I'll admit you're a better player and I'll never bother you again. But if I beat you, you have to agree to meet with me one day a week for one hour. And you have to start going to church with me every Sunday."

His mouth dropped open. He stood processing my challenge for a few seconds, then shot me a cocky smirk. "I'm not worried," he said. "There's no way you're going to beat me!"

I reached into my bag and slowly pulled my paddle from its leather case with my left hand. As I lined up on my side of the table, we began warming up with a few practice shots. He won the first point, I won the next two, then he stepped up his game and won a couple more. It seemed that we were pretty evenly matched.

Finally he said, "Okay, Stump. Time to play."

I nodded in agreement, but before setting up I said, "I just have one quick question. You don't mind if I play with my good hand now, do you?"

With that I switched the paddle to my right hand and motioned for him to serve. His face turned white and his mouth dropped open.

I beat him 21–1.

I'm not sure if it was respect or humiliation that got him to our first meeting, but Andrew held true to his promise. He began meeting with me once a week for an hour, each time opening up the Bible and studying the claims of Jesus. Andrew wasn't a believer, but he was sincerely curious about the person of Jesus. So we studied him together. It was only a few short weeks into our meetings that he decided to surrender his life and heart to Jesus.

He started going to church with me every week and became a serious student of the Bible. Every time we met, he came with more questions about Jesus, and we'd explore those questions together. It was exciting to see him growing in his faith.

Andrew and I became the best of friends during his years at Stanford. I watched him become one of the team's most outspoken believers and a guest speaker at outreach events. He encouraged several of his teammates to start meeting with me, and most of them became believers as well.

Andrew went on to have a successful career in professional football, playing for three different NFL teams. Throughout his professional life he continued to be an outspoken believer and role model to young people.

The Joy of Mentoring

The summer before his senior year, I invited Andrew and one of the other athletes I was mentoring to accompany me on a mission trip to Alaska. While there, we spoke at a number of youth camps, churches, and native Alaskan villages. We also used the time to get in some good fishing for king salmon on the Kenai River, close to where I was raised.

Each morning we would spend time in prayer and Bible study before heading out for the day. We also read a chapter each day from Randy Alcorn's great book *The Grace and Truth Paradox*, then spent a little time discussing what we'd read. It was a fruitful trip. Not only did we get to spend quality time together, but a lot of young people were brought to the Lord through the testimonies of Andrew and the other athletes traveling with us.

I'll never forget the great time of worship and conversation we had one evening on the shores of Lake Iliamna as we watched the sun set over Alaska's largest body of fresh water. I planned to have a communion service right there on the lake, with magnificent, snow-capped mountains towering above us on every side. I remember reflecting on the first time I met Andrew, and how different a man he was today than he was that day at the Ping-Pong table nearly four years earlier. God had done an amazing work in his heart and life, and I was honored that he had allowed me to play a small mentoring role in Andrew's transformation. He was committed to the process of becoming a mature man of God.

On the plane ride home, Andrew turned to me and said, "You know, Jim, I think I've learned more in the last ten days than I have in the last four years of college." I understood what he meant.

There are times when I have to pinch myself just to make sure I'm not dreaming. It's impossible to verbalize the joy and satisfaction that God continually brings into my life by having allowed me to be a spiritual mentor at Stanford for the last forty-plus years.

Andrew is just one of many, *many* students I've been privileged to meet and mentor in the Christian faith, and that thought thrills me beyond words. As a campus minister, I get to help people find their new life in Jesus. And as a spiritual mentor, I'm able to help people grow and flourish in their walk with the Lord. Those are two roles that I take very seriously.

More than that, they are two roles that I've learned to combine into an effective method of identifying and growing disciples of Jesus. The method is not one that is unique to me, and it's not rocket science. In fact, it's an idea that comes right from the pages of Scripture, directly from the life of Jesus. Yet I'm surprised how novel the idea seems to so many believers.

One Individual at a Time

Billy Graham was once asked during an interview, "If you were a pastor of a large church in a principal city, what would be your plan of action?"

Without hesitation, Dr. Graham answered, "I think one of the first things I would do would be to get a small group of eight or ten or twelve people around me that would meet a few hours a week and pay the price! It would cost them something in time and effort. I would share with them everything I have, over a period of years. Then I would actually have twelve ministers among the laypeople who in turn could take eight or ten or twelve more and teach them. . . . Christ, I think, set the pattern. He spent most of his time with twelve men. He didn't spend it with great crowds."[1]

It was an interesting answer from a man who had spent much of his life and ministry speaking to large crowds. I can't think of one person who has had a greater impact on the world for Jesus than Billy Graham—at least in the twentieth century. Countless thousands have come to Christ at his large group meetings. Yet even he understood that true disciples are built not from a pulpit but one-on-one, in small, intimate settings. I am convinced that if pastors of churches around the world would just take Billy Graham's advice and begin mentoring assistant pastors and elders, who go on to mentor other leaders in their churches, then the first-century spiritual explosion would happen all over again in this age!

The Discipling Model

When Jesus saw Peter and Andrew fishing in the Sea of Galilee, he said to them, "Come, follow me, . . . and I will send you out to fish for people" (Matt. 4:19). Immediately they left their nets and followed him.

The next day Jesus saw James and John in a boat, preparing their nets to fish, and he gave them the same invitation. They, too, immediately left their boats and their father and followed him (vv. 21–22). Soon afterward he saw Matthew sitting at a tax collector's booth and said to him, "Follow me" (Matt. 9:9). Matthew left everything behind to become a disciple of Jesus.

I'm convinced that each of the men Jesus called understood the commitment they were making when they agreed to follow him. They knew that he wasn't just asking for a few days or weeks of their time. And he wasn't simply asking them to travel with him on his journeys.

Jesus was inviting them to become his disciples. His mentorees. He was welcoming them into his inner circle. He was agreeing to become their rabbi and inviting them to become his followers.

This was a staggering opportunity for working-class Jews. At the time, every Jewish boy grew up studying the Torah and was expected to have the Pentateuch memorized by the time he was twelve. But only the best and brightest students were allowed to continue their education. Young boys who showed promise would often seek out a rabbi to teach them further, and they would ask permission to become an intimate protégé of the rabbi they most respected.

If the rabbi agreed, he would ask the young boy to follow him and become his disciple. This was a huge honor, and those who were mentored by a rabbi would usually go on to become rabbis themselves. But only a small percentage of Jewish boys were chosen for such a privilege.

The men Jesus picked were obviously not among the best and brightest students, and they might even have been rejected by rabbis as young boys. That's why they found themselves making a living as common laborers.

When Jesus, an up-and-coming young rabbi, came to them and said, "Follow me," they jumped at the chance to become his disciples. For some of them, it might have been their chance to recapture a dream they had left behind or to continue the education they were forced to abandon as children.

Jesus was asking them to leave behind everything they had worked for and to throw their entire lives into learning what he had to teach them. They weren't just giving up their careers for him; they were giving their lives over to his will for their future.

Becoming a disciple is no small commitment, and it's not for the faint of heart. It's an unwavering decision to change the direction of your life and look to your rabbi to teach and mentor you in his ways.

Jesus ultimately handpicked twelve disciples to follow him, and they became the primary focus of his life and ministry. He taught large crowds when the opportunities arose and helped a lot of people along the way, but his primary attention was always on these twelve men.

Why he chose these twelve men is still a mystery to me. If I were a coach, I would have cut them all, based on how they're depicted in the Gospels prior to Jesus' resurrection. The fact that he kept them as disciples should give us all great assurance that he will never leave us or forsake us!

Often when the crowds got too large, Jesus would escape to a quieter place to be alone with his disciples. He wasn't overlooking those who needed him; he just refused to let anything get in the way of his primary mission—to mold and shape a handful of men who would eventually go on not only to change the world but to have an impact that would ring well into eternity.

Our Great Commission

In the Gospels, Jesus modeled for his disciples—and for us—the perfect approach to mentoring people into a deep and meaningful faith. He poured his entire life into the lives of these few men. At the end of his mission on earth, after he had suffered on the cross and risen from the grave to defeat death once and for all, just before ascending back to heaven to be with his Father for eternity, he gave his disciples one last charge: "Therefore go and make disciples of all nations, baptizing them in the name of the Father and of the Son and of the Holy Spirit, and teaching them to obey everything I have commanded you. And surely I am with you always, to the very end of the age" (Matt. 28:19–20).

He didn't say to them, "Go preach about me," or "Go share the Good News," or even "Go build a megachurch in every city."

What he said was, "Go and make disciples."

Jesus commissioned them to go into the world and replicate the model of mentoring that they had learned from him. He was saying to them, "Now you are the rabbis, so go and disciple others, just the way I discipled you."

His desire was to see the Good News about him spread throughout the entire world, and for his church to grow into an unstoppable force for God among the nations. He longed to see lives transformed by his message of salvation. His ultimate desire was for every person on earth to hear and accept the message that he loved them and wanted an ongoing love relationship with them.

The apostle Peter tells us, "The Lord is not slow in keeping his promise, as some understand slowness. Instead he is patient with you, not wanting anyone to perish, but everyone to come to repentance" (2 Pet. 3:9).

Jesus longs to see every person accept his offer of salvation. But he knows that kind of thing doesn't happen through great speeches or even great ideas.

You change the world by reshaping hearts and lives from the inside out. By walking with people on a daily basis, teaching them how to live by modeling a Christlike life.

You change the world one individual at a time.

This is the model of evangelism that Jesus taught, and it's the method I've given my life to pursuing. I've seen firsthand the power of the Good News when passed on to others, not through words or speeches but through reflecting the character of Jesus. Through living the gospel, not just preaching it. Through pouring my life into just a handful of people who need Jesus.

Stay with me while we explore this model together.

1

Everyone Needs the Savior

God cannot give us happiness and peace apart from Himself, because
it is not there. There is no such thing.

—C. S. Lewis

My "office" at Stanford University is a small table in the corner of Jimmy V's Sports Café. For much of the past forty-two years, this has been where I meet students on a daily basis for food and conversation. It's not a quiet office, but I love the view, and people always know where to find me.

One day recently I was gathering my things to leave when a freshman football player rushed up to my table and said, "I was just in the locker room having a conversation with some other teammates, and they were talking about having a personal relationship with Jesus. I don't even know what that is, but I'm really interested in finding out."

He went on to explain that he'd been to church before and even believed in God, but the idea of being in a personal relationship with God was completely foreign to him. "If you can show me how to become a follower of Jesus without being a hypocrite, I'm very interested," he said.

I put my things back on the table and invited him to sit down. That day marked the first of many conversations we had about Jesus. He is now a committed follower of Jesus and has also led others into a personal faith.

This scene may sound like a rare occurrence, but it's actually far more common than you might expect. In my years of mentoring athletes at Stanford University, I've had thousands of conversations about Jesus with students, and I seldom run across anyone who isn't interested in at least talking about him. Jesus is a fascinating historical figure, and even those who have given little thought to Jesus have many questions about who he was, what he taught, and why people are still talking about him two thousand years later.

I've run across numerous people who are turned off by Christians, but I can count on one hand those who aren't at least curious about the person of Jesus.

People Long to Know

The fact that most people are curious about Jesus is a truth I discovered during my first few months at Stanford. It was 1970, and Campus Crusade for Christ had assigned me to reach out to students at Stanford University. One of the first talks I gave, at the request of the coach, was to the freshman football players, which was a huge honor for me. My talk was brief and simple. I discussed what it means to become a follower of Jesus, and I gave examples of other athletes who had given up control of their lives to Christ and the positive impact that decision had made on their lives and careers. During the talk I remember wondering if anyone was even listening.

The very next day, while meeting with one of the school's tennis players, a young man approached me and asked, "Would you please help me? I'm really frustrated right now!"

I remembered his face from the previous afternoon's meeting. He was one of the freshman football players. "Absolutely," I told him. "What can I help you with?"

He told me that my talk had made such an impact on him that after the meeting he went looking for a friend he knew to be a Christian. He and this friend lived in the same dorm, just down the hall from each other. He told his friend about my talk and said, "I'm very interested in becoming a follower of Jesus. Would you show me how?"

He said his friend seemed startled but encouraged him in his quest. Yet he wasn't much help. "He told me that becoming a Christian was the best thing he had ever done and that it really helped him. But then he just turned and walked away."

I could see why he was frustrated.

After that incident he decided to take a walk on campus and soon ran into a girl from one of his classes. He had once heard her talk about a regular Bible study on campus that she attended, so he asked her the same question. "I'm interested in becoming a follower of Jesus," he said, "but I don't know how. Could you help me?"

Once again, the response he got was vague and noncommittal. She told him how much her faith had meant to her, encouraged him to start reading the Bible, and then hurried off to meet a friend for dinner.

His shoulders drooped in frustration as he relayed the story. "I really want to do this," he told me, "but no one seems to be able to tell me how."

That afternoon, he and I got together for our first meeting. At the end of the hour we prayed together as he invited Jesus into his life and began the incredible journey of being a follower of Jesus.

Two Universal Truths

In my many years of mentoring, I've discovered two truths that appear to be universal, and together they are reflective of one of the greatest ironies of the human condition.

The first truth is that, given the right circumstances, every person on the planet is open to hearing the story of Jesus. It is the most compelling story in the universe, and his message of hope is as fascinating as it is life-altering. Even those who say they are angry with God, when approached by someone who is genuinely interested in them, will at least listen.

And the second truth I've learned is that every sincere follower of Jesus has a deep desire to share their faith with others. They are quick to say that developing a personal relationship with Jesus is the best thing that has ever happened to them. They understand that Jesus, through his death on the cross, is the only road to salvation, and they've experienced the joy of knowing him firsthand, so they truly want to share Christ with their friends. They simply don't know how.

The irony would be laughable if it weren't so sad.

As Christians we hold in our hearts the answer to the most gut-wrenching, soul-searching questions in the universe. We know things that every human soul is longing to discover. Through the life and teachings of Jesus, we know things about life and death and eternity that have confounded philosophers since the beginning of time.

Because of our faith in Jesus, you and I know the truth of creation, the purpose of our existence, the fate of humanity, and the one and only true meaning of life. Not only do we know who we are and why we were made, but we also know what's going to happen after we die. Because of Jesus, our eternal fate is sealed and certain and exciting beyond comprehension!

Who wouldn't want to know that?

We should be excited to share Jesus with everyone. But instead we find ourselves keeping silent, afraid to bring up our faith for fear of sounding judgmental or making others feel awkward.

Statistics show that 95 percent of all Christians have never helped another person find a relationship with Jesus. It's a sobering statistic, and many might chalk it up to apathy, but I don't think that's true. I'm convinced it's because most of those 95 percent simply don't know what to say or how to say it.

God's *Real* Business

Because of my role on campus, I get invited to a lot of Christian functions, and often the conversation will turn to the subject of sharing your faith. When people learn that I do that for a living, they will say things like, "I really admire what you do," or "I wish I knew how to effectively share my faith with others." Sometimes they'll ask for pointers or wonder if I have some secret formula or process. They all seem curious about my methods and fascinated by the idea of regularly leading people to Jesus.

I'm always happy to share what I know, and I'm encouraged that so many Christians seem truly interested in knowing how to bring others to Christ. But a huge part of me is sad that what I do seems like such an anomaly among believers. I'm only doing what Jesus commanded every believer to do.

The hard reality is, sharing our faith with others is not a choice or a special "gift" that some Christians happen to have. It's what God expects of every follower of Jesus.

After Jesus conquered death and rose from the grave, he made several appearances to his disciples and followers, and he used that time to impart his final wishes before ascending back to heaven.

> Therefore go and make disciples of all nations, baptizing them in the name of the Father and of the Son and of the Holy Spirit, and

teaching them to obey everything I have commanded you. (Matt. 28:19–20)

He said to them, "Go into all the world and preach the gospel to all creation." (Mark 16:15)

He told them, "This is what is written: The Messiah will suffer and rise from the dead on the third day, and repentance for the forgiveness of sins will be preached in his name to all nations, beginning at Jerusalem." (Luke 24:46–47)

You and I know these statements as the Great Commission, and they are far more than a few passing words of encouragement from Jesus. They are also not suggestions—they are direct commands. They are specific instructions to believers about what it means to be a follower of Christ. Jesus left little doubt about his expectations of those who choose to believe. And his words should reflect the burden we have in our hearts for those who are lost.

C. S. Lewis once said, "The salvation of human souls . . . is the real business of life."[2] Sadly, most Christians have never taken God's "real business" to heart.

Good News!

My goal here is not to cause believers to hang their heads in shame but to mobilize God's people to action. If you've found yourself identifying with the 95 percent who have never led a friend to Jesus, please know that my intent is not to shame or discourage you. In fact, it's the exact opposite.

I have good news about sharing the Good News! It's not as hard or frightening as you've been led to believe. And most people are far more receptive to Jesus than you probably expect. They may not be interested in religion, Christianity, the Bible, or church, but they want to know about Jesus.

Sharing your faith is like riding a bike. If you've never done it, the idea sounds terrifying. And your mind tends to focus on all the negative things that might happen. *What if I fall off? What if I can't go fast enough? What if I go too fast and can't stop?*

Fear of the unknown causes unnecessary anxiety. Once we get started and actually find our balance, we discover how exhilarating riding a bike can be. With the wind in our hair and our feet safely on the pedals, we suddenly find ourselves enjoying the view and wondering why it took us so long to try and seemed so scary.

The same is true about sharing our faith. Most believers haven't led a friend to Jesus simply because they haven't taken the first step. Their mind races with all the negative things that might happen. *What if they think I'm weird? What if I say the wrong thing? What if I can't answer their questions? What if they say no?*

Fear of the unknown causes anxiety in our spirit. And we give up before ever putting our feet on the pedals.

I'm here to tell you that the exhilaration of the ride is worth overcoming even your greatest fears. That if you can just move beyond your anxiety and take the first step, you'll soon find yourself wondering why it took you so long to try.

The apostle Paul wrote, "For the Spirit God gave us does not make us timid, but gives us power, love and self-discipline. So do not be ashamed of the testimony about our Lord" (2 Tim. 1:7–8).

There is no greater experience on earth than leading another person to faith. There's nothing more rewarding than introducing a friend to Jesus and then seeing that friend accept him as their personal Lord and Savior. To pray with them for the very first time and then walk with them as they grow deeper in their relationship with Jesus.

If there's a greater rush on the planet, I certainly haven't found it. And trust me, you won't either!

Fishing for Souls

I was raised in a log cabin that my father built in the wilds of Alaska. My parents were missionaries, but in high school and college I spent most summers working as a commercial fisherman. I learned early in life the allure of fighting the ocean elements, hauling in huge nets full of sockeye salmon onto a small fishing boat, and struggling against gale-force winds and white-capped waves to transport the haul back to market. It was a grueling and exhausting job, but deeply rewarding.

One of the greatest lessons I learned during those years is that fishing is a learned skill. There are some techniques that work and others that don't. Some boats return to shore bursting at the seams with fresh fish, while others come back empty. Sometimes that result is due to unavoidable circumstances, but often it's simply a lack of acquired skill or poor planning that makes the difference. It's a harsh reality of life on the Alaskan docks. Some fishermen eat well, while others go home hungry.

That same dynamic holds true when sharing your faith. Again, there are some techniques that work and others that don't. It's easy to find yourself coming back empty-handed if you haven't taken the time to develop the right skills or methods.

Whether fishing for salmon or bringing people to Jesus, you have to learn where to cast your net and how quickly to bring it in. It's a skill that anyone can learn. But like any skill, it takes willingness, time, diligence, and patience in order to be consistently successful.

I love that Jesus used the analogy of fishing when teaching his disciples how to reach others. "Follow me," he told them, "and I will send you out to fish for people" (Matt. 4:19). It's a comparison that rings true to me, because I've experienced both of those fishing careers firsthand.

In my years as a mentor, I have always been open to looking at more effective ways to communicate the message. Anytime a new book or DVD series on how to share your faith hits the market, I'm one of the first to check it out and see what it has to say. When it comes to leading others to Jesus, I want to be as effective as possible, so I glean what I can from others. And what I've learned is that not all techniques are created equal. Some will bring you joy and success, while others will leave you feeling frustrated and insecure.

I don't like being frustrated, and as a man who stands just five feet three inches tall—with the last name of Stump, no less—I have had many people try to make me feel insecure. I want to spend my time and energy on something that works, and I'm sure you do too.

Knowing What Works

The nonprofit ministry I oversee at Stanford is called Sports Challenge, and our primary focus is reaching out to student athletes on campus. I left Campus Crusade for Christ in 1974 in order to form Sports Challenge, an independent 501(c)(3) organization, because I wanted to focus my ministry specifically on mentoring student athletes on the Stanford campus. The reason I chose student athletes is that I grew up playing sports and played several sports in college, so athletes are the people I most easily relate to as a group.

The success I have had helping student athletes begin a relationship with Jesus has gotten a lot of attention from other ministries. (When I say *success*, I simply mean sharing with another person how they can begin a relationship with Jesus, trusting in the power of the Holy Spirit, and leaving the results to God.) My success is not because I happen to be some superevangelist or silver-tongued salesman. I am not the most charismatic individual on campus by a long shot. Yet God has blessed me beyond belief with fruit for the kingdom.

In fact, just over a year ago, I was approached by the director of a major sports ministry at Stanford, and he asked if he could attend our next board meeting at Sports Challenge. "I have some information I think your board of directors needs to know," he told me.

I wasn't sure what he meant or whether I should be worried, but I invited him to come. At the meeting, he explained to our board that for some time he had been tracking the results of all the evangelical groups on campus, and what he found was surprising. "There are around twenty evangelical campus ministries here at Stanford," he said, "and we've discovered that Jim Stump leads more students to Christ each year than all those other campus ministries combined."

You could have knocked me over with a feather. I'm familiar with a lot of the other campus ministries, and many of them have great programs and outreach events for students. They're making a huge impact for the kingdom in their own way, and I thank God for the work they do and the fact that I can be in the trenches with them. They encourage me with their faithfulness, so I don't give this fact to boast or to downplay the efforts of others. Sharing the Good News is not a competitive sport. I bring it up only to show that we're clearly doing something right. Even though we're one of the smallest outreach ministries on campus, we've been able to see great things happen to expand the kingdom. I'm excited to see God use our faithful efforts in such a powerful way.

And it confirms for me what I've always believed: no matter how godless our society becomes, no matter how far our country drifts from godly principles, no matter how many young people stray from the truth, the gospel message is still the most compelling, life-changing story in the universe. And God's principles, when communicated in the right way, with the right spirit, can stir even the coldest and darkest heart to turn from the direction they are going and follow him.

Living the Gospel

So what makes the difference? What method or program are we using at Sports Challenge to bring about such surprising results when it comes to helping students begin a relationship with Jesus?

Quite frankly, I wish I had a fancy name for it. Maybe then I could package and patent it. But the truth is, what we do is not that unique or complicated. It's a principle of sharing your faith that is so simple and effective that I'm surprised it isn't taught and practiced by every follower of Jesus!

My approach to evangelism is the same approach that Jesus used two thousand years ago. I call it simply *mentoring people to Jesus*.

When Jesus walked the earth, ministering to the sick and bringing hope to the lost, his life and his message were indistinguishable. In fact, his life *was* his message. He shared the truth by sharing himself.

Jesus made no distinction between evangelizing and discipling. They were one and the same. He brought people to himself through mentoring.

Too often we see the Good News as a block of information that we're supposed to share with others. We try to win people for Jesus by relaying words and principles from the Bible. Our focus is on convincing people that they need God and then leading them through the sinner's prayer. Then we make a check by their name and move on to the next person who might be looking for answers in their life.

But the Good News isn't a principle or a concept. It's a lifestyle. It's a living, breathing entity of hope and salvation. And the most effective way to relay the Good News of Jesus is to live it. To *be* the message, not just preach it. That's what Jesus did. And that's what I try to do.

When Jesus set out to choose his twelve disciples—twelve men who would one day be the leaders of those who would spread his message throughout the entire earth—he approached them with one simple request: "Follow me."

"Walk with me," he was telling them. "Watch me. Learn from me. Let me show you how to live."

Jesus understood that the only way to truly gain someone's heart is by first gaining their trust. And that's what mentoring is all about. It's about sharing God's message of hope by sharing yourself.

Evangelism through Mentoring

This book is my attempt to further explore this concept of sharing your faith through mentoring and to relay the principles I've learned. I don't believe in simply leading others to Jesus; I believe in mentoring them to Jesus and then helping them fall in love with him.

The ideas and concepts we'll discuss are the culmination of nearly a half century of learning and listening, of trial and error, of success and failure along the way. It's my humble attempt to pass on to others what God has graciously imparted to me.

And the fact that you've found yourself on this page indicates volumes about your heart and spirit. It tells me that you are not an apathetic believer. That you are not taking your salvation lightly. That you care deeply about those who don't yet know Jesus personally, and you possess a powerful burden in your spirit to share the gospel message with others.

It tells me that you have a friend who needs to find that personal relationship with Jesus, and that you want to be the conduit through which the Holy Spirit brings them to a place where they desire to become a follower of Jesus.

It appears that we have a common bond, you and I, so let's begin this journey together.

PART 1

The Mentoring Model
of Sharing Your Faith

What we want is to win souls. They are not won by flowery speeches.

—Charles Spurgeon

It is not primarily out of compassion for humanity that we share our faith or pray for the lost; it is first of all, love for God.

—John Piper

Follow my example, as I follow the example of Christ.

—1 Corinthians 11:1

2

The Accidental Evangelist

How beautiful are the feet of those who bring good news!

—Romans 10:15

Growing up in the wilds of Alaska was a great adventure. Several miles from our log cabin, the Iliamna River flowed out of the mountains and down to Lake Iliamna, the largest lake in Alaska. Just upriver from the bridge that crossed the river was a huge eagle's nest, and the native Indian elders told me tales about how the eagle families functioned. The young eaglets would bounce and chirp in their nest, begging for food, as the majestic male scoured the earth below, looking for morsels of meat.

Often he'd spy a pack of seagulls fighting over a dead salmon. Like a heat-seeking missile he would begin to dive, plunging toward the earth at breakneck speed. Then just before reaching the ground, he'd spread his massive wings and extend his powerful claws downward. The frightened seagulls would scatter like cockroaches as he grabbed the half-eaten carcass out from under them and carried it back to the nest. It was an amazing sight to behold.

But even more fascinating was hearing how eagles teach their young to fly. When an eaglet is only a few weeks old, barely big enough to stand on its own, its mother gently nudges it toward the edge of the nest with her beak. Then without warning she pushes it out of the nest. The young eaglet screams and squawks in fear as it tumbles end over end, hurtling toward the earth. Instinctively it flaps its untested wings, struggling desperately to slow its fall.

Just before it reaches the rocks below, the mother swoops beneath it, catching the young eaglet on the back of her wings, then carries it back to the nest.

Before the frightened bird can even catch its breath, the mother repeats the scenario. Again the eaglet screams and frantically flaps its young wings, fighting to survive the fall. And once again the mother catches it at the last minute and carries it back to the nest.

Time after time the mother eagle repeats this process, until eventually the exhausted young eaglet learns to fly on its own power.

It's a rite of passage that every eaglet has to endure. I often wondered what those poor eaglets felt as they hurtled helplessly toward the earth, awkwardly wrestling to find their wings before being crushed by the rocks.

It never occurred to me at the time that I would someday experience firsthand what that terrifying free fall must have been like.

Out of Alaska

It was two days after my twenty-second birthday when I finally surrendered and gave my heart and life to Jesus.

Surprising, since I had grown up going to church. In fact, our small congregation met in the front room of our log cabin, so I never missed a service. I was the second son of full-time Christian missionaries. My parents were godly people who threw their entire lives into serving the Lord, yet somehow I had never internalized the faith they tried to instill in me. I knew all the right words and Christian terminology and had even memorized many of the verses that believers are supposed to know. I was the ultimate Christian poser. I knew a lot about Jesus and the Bible; I simply could not figure out how it all applied to my life from a practical perspective.

And I was good at not embarrassing my parents. You could have asked anyone in our village about me, and they would readily testify that I was a "good Christian kid." Yet in my heart, I had no personal relationship with Jesus. I knew a lot *about* him, but I didn't know him.

Out of high school I was accepted into Wheaton College, and I was thrilled to go. Wheaton had the reputation of being the "Stanford" of Christian colleges, having the best combination of academics and athletics in Division III colleges. My goal was to become a high school coach, so it seemed like the perfect place for me.

I excelled at Wheaton and quickly became a popular figure on campus. Most of my time was spent playing sports, which had always been my passion. I also developed my game as a table tennis player, defeating several state champions and winning the Wheaton College championship all four years I was there.

At the end of my junior year, I was elected to a student body office that placed me in charge of orientation for the incoming freshmen. I was excited when I first heard about my responsibilities, because I loved being in a leadership role on campus. I also thought about all those freshman girls who would need help finding their way around school. *Now this is a job I can handle*, I thought.

But it wasn't long before I realized the real weight of the responsibility. I was about to become potentially the first person freshmen would come to when they had questions about life and faith and God, and I had no idea how I was going to pull it off. Though I had promised myself that I would seek out answers to life's deepest questions when I entered Wheaton, I had never actually dealt with most of those questions. I knew that I was the last guy those students needed to be asking, because I didn't have the answers.

Senior Year

That summer before my senior year, while working as a commercial fisherman in Bristol Bay, Alaska, I found myself struggling with anxiety. How could I answer questions from incoming freshmen that I had never even dealt with myself?

I decided to get serious. Maybe if I started going back to church and reading my Bible every day, I'd be able to catch the faith that my parents had. Maybe somehow it would all begin to make sense. Maybe I could do what I had always done—fake it, until someday I just might make it.

And that's exactly what I did. I went back to school with a renewed determination. I started reading my Bible each day and attending church every Sunday. And when freshmen came to me with questions, I did my best to give them a good biblical answer. I actually didn't find it that difficult. I'd spent most of my life as a poser, so I knew all the right Christian lingo. I even quoted Bible verses from memory. *Just like riding a bike*, I thought. Yet for all my efforts, nothing was really different. In my heart I knew I was still just pretending.

Then one day a girl I was dating invited me to attend an event sponsored by Campus Crusade. I honestly didn't want to go, until I found out that the speaker had been a five-time West Coast handball champion and had been student body president at the University of Oregon. I had always respected and admired the accomplishments of successful people, so it didn't take much convincing for me to go.

The speaker's name was Bud Hinkson, and I was fascinated by his personal story and his vision to impact the world. He was recruiting a team of several dozen college graduates who would train here in the States for a year and then travel to Europe to talk to university students about Jesus.

As Bud spoke, it became obvious that he seemed to know God in a way that was completely foreign to me. I was envious of the way he talked about Jesus and the relationship he seemed to have. I had tried as a child to develop that kind of friendship with Jesus, but it never seemed to come. *What does he know that I don't know?* I thought.

Afterward, while people were mingling and visiting, I remained in my chair, thinking about what he had said, and I found myself feeling frustrated and alone. *Why can't I find the kind of relationship with Jesus that Bud spoke about? What am I doing wrong?*

At that moment I looked up and Bud was standing over me, his hand outstretched in my direction. I was a bit startled.

"You're Jim Stump, aren't you?" he asked.

"Yes," I told him, surprised that he knew my name.

"I've heard about you."

I stood and shook his hand, wondering who he had been talking to and what he'd heard.

"I would like to invite you to lunch tomorrow and talk to you about joining this team that I'm putting together," he told me.

As a college student, whenever anyone offered a free lunch, I was all over it. So I quickly took him up on his offer.

As we got to know each other throughout the course of lunch, Bud said, "I'm looking for men like you to join me this summer in San Bernardino, California. Campus Crusade is sponsoring a staff-training event, and the rest of the team members will be there. I'll pay your way and you can work with us this summer. We can talk about your experience at the end of the summer, and if this ends up being something that doesn't work for you, you can be back to graduate school in the fall. Give it a try and see what you think."

To this day, I'm not sure why I agreed to go. I had my future completely planned out, and working with a ministry like Campus Crusade was nowhere on the list. But Bud was a compelling figure, and I wanted to get to know him better. I wanted to find out what made him the man that he appeared to be.

So I hesitantly agreed, having no idea why, or what I was going to find in Southern California. *He's willing to pay my way*, I thought. *I might as well enjoy the free vacation!*

A Journey Begins

I arrived in San Bernardino on July 17, 1966, my twenty-second birthday. And just two nights later I found myself at an orientation event at the Campus Crusade headquarters.

As the speaker that night shared his testimony on how he had found true meaning in a relationship with Jesus, I found myself moved in a way that I hadn't experienced before. I had heard hundreds, maybe thousands of sermons in my life, yet I had never heard the story of Jesus the way this man presented it. I found myself fighting back tears during his entire talk, struggling to keep my composure. I had never quite comprehended the depth and breadth of God's unconditional love and the role that the Holy Spirit played in the life of a Christian. That night, after the meeting ended, I left the building, sat down under a palm tree, and prayed a prayer that I never had before.

I asked God to forgive me for the many years I had been pretending to be a follower of Jesus, and I pleaded for him to come into my life and make me whole. I told him I was tired of posing and was ready to become a true follower of Jesus. I asked him to come into my heart and change me from the inside out, to heal the brokenness in my spirit, and to give me the strength to stay faithful to his Word. I asked him to save me and to make me a new creation. Then I took the step of faith of thanking him for coming in as he had promised.

That night I felt a profound calmness in my spirit, something I hadn't felt in twenty-two years. For the first time in my life, I was at peace! I felt God's presence in a way I'd never thought possible. I experienced his grace and mercy. I embraced his love and acceptance.

I knew my life would never again be the same.

I went back to my room that night and began reading my Bible, beginning in the book of John, and it was as if I were reading the stories for the very first time. Scripture suddenly came alive to me. As I read the story of Jesus, he no longer seemed like an elusive and distant historical figure. He was genuine and tangible and mesmerizing. He was a real and personal friend.

San Bernardino

When I woke the next morning, I couldn't wait to get back to the staff training. My mind was still reeling from the previous night, and I prayed again to my new friend, renewing my vow to follow him no matter where he led. I had a fresh lift in my spirit and a spring in my step as I found a seat close to the front of the room.

But my exuberance quickly turned to apprehension. I was expecting another encouraging challenge, but instead the speaker said, "Today we're going to learn how to lead someone into a personal relationship with Jesus, then we're going to put what we've learned into practice. We're going to go down to Huntington Beach and share our faith with others."

He spent twenty minutes going over a few tips and principles of how to share our faith, and then he gave us each a handful of small booklets titled *The Four Spiritual Laws*.[3] He instructed us to go back to our rooms, grab some sunscreen and a beach towel, and meet him in the front parking lot.

I was terrified. I had never once shared my faith with another person. I'd only been a sincere follower for about twelve hours myself, and now I was supposed to help others find what had been so elusive for me for so many years? I had no idea what to say or do. I tried to think of a way to get out of it, but before I knew it we were all crammed into buses, heading toward the beach. I began to pray for a Los Angeles traffic jam so that we wouldn't make it to the beach, but God seemed to have other plans.

As we drove along the freeways of Southern California, the engine noise droning in the background, I could feel sweat dripping down my forehead. I found my mind drifting back to my days as a child, listening to how those poor eaglets were pushed out of their comfortable nest, tumbled toward the earth, and struggled to keep from crashing onto the rocks below. For the first time, I got a small taste of what that experience must have been like.

I glanced down at the booklets in my hand and noticed that my knuckles were beginning to turn white. I wondered what the others were going to say when they discovered that I was completely unprepared for what was about to come. Everyone else seemed so calm and collected, even excited, to begin talking to these total strangers, and it was all I could do to keep from passing out.

Dear Lord, what have I gotten myself into? Please give me the strength to get through this. Please catch me before I crash onto the rocks below.

Meeting God at the Beach

The man sitting next to me on the bus must have sensed my concern, because he asked if I wanted to tag along with him once we got there. His name was Steve, and he had been a baseball player at the University of California at Berkeley. He told me he'd been training with Campus Crusade for about six months and was willing to give me pointers and help me get started. "Don't worry," he said. "It's not as frightening as it sounds once you get going."

I was thrilled at his offer. *Thank you, Jesus*, I prayed silently.

We were each given a pencil and a clipboard with a questionnaire titled "National Collegiate Religious Survey." We were instructed to use the survey as a means of breaking the ice when talking to people on the beach. We were to find people close to our age and ask if they'd be willing to help with the survey. The last question on the survey was, "If you could know God personally, would you be interested?" If the answer was yes, we were to use the *Four Spiritual Laws* booklet to share the message of Jesus with them. I had never seen the booklet before that morning.

When we reached the beach, Steve told me to stay by his side as we looked for someone to talk to. We had gone less than fifty yards when he found the perfect candidate, a young man in his late teens, tanned and shirtless, sitting on a bench near the ocean.

"You don't have to do anything," Steve told me. "Just watch me and listen to what I say. It's really pretty simple."

We approached the young man, and Steve asked if he'd be willing to help us out with a survey we were conducting. "It will just take a few minutes," he said.

The young man agreed, and Steve began going over the questions, writing the man's answers as he went. After the young man answered yes to the last question, Steve thanked him for helping and asked, "Have you ever heard of the four spiritual laws?"

"No," the man said. But he seemed intrigued.

Steve began reading through the booklet, going over the points one by one. The four principles were designed to clearly present the message of how to begin a relationship with Jesus. I was surprised by how attentive the man seemed to be.

But before Steve could finish, another young man sauntered up to us. He had been body surfing and noticed us talking to his friend, so he came to see what was going on.

Steve turned to me and said, "Jim, why don't you take this man down the beach and see if he can help with our survey?" Then he turned to the newcomer and asked, "You don't mind helping us out, do you?"

"Sure," the friend said, his hair still dripping wet from the ocean.

I'm sure my eyes were wide as saucers, but I couldn't turn back now. I took the young friend a few yards down the beach, found a quiet place to sit in the sand, and stumbled my way through the survey, penciling in his comments as he answered each question.

When I came to the last question, I took a deep breath and read it aloud. "If you could know God personally, would you be interested?"

"I guess so," he answered. I was almost hoping he would say no and was astonished that he actually said yes! So I awkwardly took out the *Four Spiritual Laws* booklet and began to read. The more I read, the more intently he seemed to listen.

When I got to the fourth principle, I quoted Jesus' commitment to us in Revelation 3:20: "Here I am! I stand at the door and knock. If anyone hears my voice and opens the door, I will come in and eat with that person, and they with me."

Then I looked up, swallowed hard, and mustered the courage to ask, "Have you ever opened the door and asked Jesus to come in?"

"No, I haven't," he answered. "No one has ever told me how. But I'd like to. Can we do that right now?"

I can't remember the last time I felt so stunned. "Sure, we can pray right now," I told him.

Right then and there we bowed our heads and prayed together. He repeated my words as I led him in a prayer to invite Jesus into his heart and accept God's gift of eternal life. As we finished, he looked up and a tear was running down his face. His heart was truly broken, his words genuine.

I took down his name and phone number, then told him that I would be in touch soon to help him find a church and to answer any questions he might have. Then I hurried down the beach to tell Steve what had happened. My heart was bursting with joy. I had never experienced such thrill and excitement.

Steve smiled as I shared the story with him. "I told you it wasn't that hard," he said.

I was on such a spiritual high that I immediately took off down the beach and soon found another young man tanning on a chair by the ocean. I introduced myself to him and asked if he'd be willing to help with our survey. He agreed, so once again I took out the questionnaire and went over it with him. Afterward I asked if I could explain the four spiritual laws to him, and again he agreed.

His response was so similar it was frightening. As I read the final principle, I asked if he had ever opened the door of his life and invited Jesus to come in, and he answered, "No, but I'd really like to." Then I knelt down and prayed with him as he asked Jesus into his heart to become his Lord and Savior.

I couldn't believe how open people were to the message of Jesus. I'd never imagined that so many were eager to hear the Good News. And that they would be so quick to respond to God's offer of salvation.

A Simple Prayer

We all have moments in our lives that forever define the direction of our future. They are moments that come in an instant, almost always unexpectedly, and once played out, they completely redirect the course of our lives.

These moments are seldom planned and always extraordinary, and they affect our lives in a way that is unquestionably supernatural.

That day on the beach, those many years ago, marked for me such a moment. It was the most life-changing, career-altering, heart-shifting experience of my existence. The thrill of feeling God's hand guide me as I walked along the beach, sharing the story of Jesus with others, testifying about God's grace and goodness, silently praying for wisdom as I sought out lost and searching souls, was unlike anything I had ever dreamed or imagined.

On the bus ride home that evening, I knew my life would never again be the same. Something deep in my spirit was stirred that day. Something real and substantial. I realized that God had a plan and purpose for my life that was far different from the one I'd always had for myself.

My plan was to finish the summer in California and then head back to Illinois for graduate school in the fall. I was committed to chasing my dream of becoming a high school coach, and I was just a few short years from achieving that goal.

But God obviously had other plans. I didn't know at the time what his plan was or where it would take me, only that I was ready and willing to follow.

Dear God, I prayed silently, *I want so much to serve you. I love leading people to Jesus. Use me, Lord. I'll go wherever you want me to go. I'll do whatever you want me to do. I am yours until my dying day.*

It was a simple prayer, as honest as any words I'd ever uttered. And it was the first step toward the most extraordinary and unexpected journey of my life.

A journey that I would soon discover was almost as challenging—and demanding—as it was rewarding.

3

The Jesus Model

As Jesus walked beside the Sea of Galilee, he saw Simon and his brother Andrew casting a net into the lake, for they were fishermen. "Come, follow me," Jesus said, "and I will send you out to fish for people." At once they left their nets and followed him.

—Mark 1:16–18

Whenever God steps in and changes the direction of our future, he often follows that act with a time of testing. He doesn't do it to see if we're up to the task, because he knows that we are. He does it in order to prepare us for the challenges to come. Sometimes God shelters us; other times he pushes us out of the nest in order to strengthen our wings.

I learned this truth early in my Christian walk, within days of turning my life and career over to God's will.

When God reached in and grabbed hold of my heart that day on Huntington Beach, I knew my life would never again be the same. I promised God I would follow wherever he chose to lead, and I was committed to keeping that promise. So I abandoned my plans to return to Illinois for graduate school in the fall and instead threw myself into the work of Campus Crusade. I didn't know where the training would take me or what God had planned for my future, but for the first time in my life I knew I was right where God wanted me to be, and the feeling was exhilarating!

But it was also frightening. And I had no way of knowing the trials I would encounter along the way.

Into the Fire

Bud Hinkson called our team of seventy the "University Ambassador Team." Campus Crusade was in the process of expanding their outreach into Europe, and we were to be the first individuals to represent the ministry there. We became known as the "Green Beret" of Campus Crusade because of all the additional training we would receive under Bud's tutelage. His goal was to groom us into a hard-core group of men and women who were prepared to take on even the hardest skeptics. He knew how educated and cynical students would be at the European universities, and he wanted to make sure we were up to the task.

In order to prepare us for that mission, Bud put us through an intensive time of training and mentoring. Our training was divided into three sessions of three months each, and the second part of our training was conducted at what was then one of the most spiritually bankrupt places in the country—the University of California at Berkeley.

We spent those three months at the Berkeley campus talking to students at every opportunity. And when we weren't on campus, we were attending training classes or studying in our rooms, learning all we could about how to effectively communicate God's love to the students.

It was a challenging few months. And not everyone we ran across was as open to hearing the gospel as the friends I had met on the beach that day in Southern California. We were able to reach a lot of students for Jesus, but we also encountered a lot of hardened hearts and closed spirits. I learned very quickly that talking to students about Jesus was not for the faint of heart.

This was early in the spring of 1967, at the height of the Free Speech Movement, and many young people were in full rebellion against anything that smacked of authority. College students all over the United States were protesting the war in Vietnam, and rebellion was running rampant among young people. The sexual revolution was in full swing, and kids were experimenting with sex and drugs and any other type of immoral behavior they could think of. If you lived through those years, you likely remember well how tumultuous things had become. It was a time of spiritual and political turmoil greater than most Americans had ever seen or imagined. And Berkeley was the epicenter of it.

And here I was, a wide-eyed twenty-two-year old, fresh from the backwoods of Alaska, thrust right into the middle of all this. Before that time my only experience away from home had been a sheltered dorm room at Wheaton College, and suddenly I found myself navigating my newfound faith in the midst of one of the most rebellious places in the nation.

And I'd thought the days of throwing Christians to the lions were over.

A Different World

I remember one night sitting in my small, first-floor apartment down the street from the Berkeley campus. I had my window open in order to let in some fresh air and could hear the sounds of talking and laughing as students headed back to their dorm rooms after another long night of partying.

At one point I heard a commotion outside and looked out the window to see what was going on. I noticed two large guys walking down the middle of the street with a young woman walking between them. They had obviously been drinking because they were talking loudly enough to wake up the entire neighborhood.

I watched as they rounded the corner of the street, then suddenly the young girl started screaming and freaking out for no apparent reason. Something in her just snapped, and she started running in circles, flailing her arms back and forth. She grabbed one of the men and flung him to the ground next to the far curb. The other man tried to restrain her, but she pushed him to the ground toward the other curb, almost as if she had superhuman strength. Then she began running up the street toward a parking garage at the end of the block.

I ran outside to make sure the men were okay, and they seemed completely stunned. They had no idea what had gotten into the girl or why she had flipped out. The three of us made our way up the street and found her huddled in a fetal position in one corner of the parking garage. She was rocking back and forth, screaming at the top of her lungs, "I hate you, God! God, I hate you!" Over and over she screamed it.

We found a nearby phone booth and called 911, then did our best to make sure she didn't hurt herself while we waited on the ambulance to arrive. One of the men confessed to me that she had been dropping LSD along with a few other drugs and was apparently having a "bad trip."

Eventually the medics arrived and took the girl to the hospital. Once the commotion died down, I made my way back to my apartment, still shaken.

The ordeal reminded me again just how out of place I felt at Berkeley. This was a world that I knew nothing about. I had never been around the kind of drugs and drinking and rebellion that I saw on a daily basis at Berkeley. In California, every day was a new experience, and each one seemed to be an even greater shock to my system.

I had always known about spiritual warfare and the dark hold that Satan had on the world, but it wasn't something I had ever given much thought to. It was just one of those spiritual things my parents used to talk about at church or warn us kids about at the dinner table. I was always more interested in sports and girls and hanging out with my friends. But now I was seeing firsthand the powerful hold that Satan had on the world, and the pain and hopelessness of living a life bound by sin and addiction.

Like all young people, I had experienced the temptations of lust and drugs and immorality as I grew up, but at Berkeley I became an eyewitness to the consequences of giving in to those temptations. And it was not a pretty sight.

Meeting Paul

That experience was just one of many spiritual battles our team faced during our time at Berkeley. Every time we approached someone with the Good News, we never knew the response we would get. Some had never heard about Jesus and were immediately open to talking about him, while others recoiled and ran the minute we brought up his name. It was obvious that Satan didn't like us there and began circling his wagons every time we came into his territory.

But that didn't stop us from talking to students and learning important lessons from each conversation. And we were able to reach a lot of hardened hearts for Jesus. One particular experience I had taught me the importance of understanding and focusing on the basics when sharing Jesus with others.

I was sitting in my apartment reading one day when a knock came at the front door. It was a young man who was a student body officer and also played on one of the varsity sports teams.

He introduced himself as Paul and said a friend of his told him he should come to see me.

Apparently his friend had heard me speak at a team meeting the previous week and thought that Paul would be interested in talking to me. Either that or he was playing a trick on me. We made small talk for a few minutes, and then he asked me, "So what are you doing on the Cal campus?"

"I'm here talking to students about the life and claims of Jesus Christ," I told him.

A puzzled look came over his face. "I have no idea who that is," he said.

I thought he was joking. "Surely you've heard about Jesus."

Again he told me, "I have no idea who he is." He went on to say that he'd heard the name, but only as an expletive that teammates would say when they got angry or missed a shot on goal.

I soon learned that Paul had been raised in a Jewish home in the Bay Area, and he honestly couldn't remember his family ever talking about Jesus. I asked him to sit down and I began sharing with him. He knew almost nothing about the Bible. His family may have been Jewish, but apparently they weren't practicing their faith. So I started from the very beginning, with the creation story, and from there began recapping the key stories of the Old Testament.

I had never seen someone so fascinated by the Scriptures. We talked all afternoon, and when it began to get dark, we set a time to meet the following week to continue talking.

Paul and I began meeting once a week to study the life of Jesus, and each time we met he seemed even more eager to learn. In the sixth week of our meeting together, I asked if he'd like to accept Jesus as his Lord and Messiah. Without hesitation he said, "Yes, I would." So the two of us bowed our heads as he invited Jesus into his life.

I've never forgotten the look in his eyes as he lifted his head to thank me. There's nothing on earth more thrilling than seeing someone give their life over to Jesus, placing their future in his hands. To see someone experience true peace and happiness for the very first time. To see a true seeker find answers in the arms of their new Lord and Savior.

Paul and I became good friends during that time, and after my training period in California ended, the two of us stayed in touch. It was exciting to see him grow in his faith and even begin sharing his relationship with Jesus with others.

A New Approach

God used that experience to teach me some important lessons about leading others to Christ. During the training period at Berkeley, most of the sharing we did was with students on campus. We would scour the places where students gathered, looking for people willing to give us a few minutes of their time, then use the material we were given to share Jesus with them. Sometimes they would allow us to pray with them, and we were always diligent to get their contact information so that someone could follow up later. But often we were not involved in that follow-up, so we never truly knew what happened with them.

With Paul that wasn't the case. He and I developed a friendship, and I was able to spend more quality time teaching and mentoring him in the faith. He had the chance to ask a lot of questions about Jesus and the Bible, and we investigated those questions together. He wasn't just another person on campus I stopped to talk with about Jesus; he became a friend I got to know on a heart-to-heart level. And I became emotionally invested in helping him discover the truths about Jesus.

I wasn't simply teaching him about Jesus; I was walking with him through the process. We explored the truths of Scripture together and developed a deeper friendship in the process. And there was something extremely rewarding about that. It just felt right. By the time he gave his life to Jesus, I knew he was ready to make that decision and he understood the implications of it. It wasn't an emotional, spur-of-the-moment decision on his part. He had all the knowledge he needed to make an informed choice, and he knew that the prayer he was about to pray would be a life-altering one.

The experience taught me that sharing your faith is about so much more than explaining the gospel to someone. It's about living the gospel. Not just telling people about Jesus but becoming the Jesus they may never again meet. As believers, we are so much more than spokesmen for Jesus; we are ambassadors of the truth. We don't just share the gospel; we illustrate it with our lives. I learned that the most effective way to bring people into a meaningful relationship with Jesus is to first show them what a meaningful relationship looks like.

This doesn't mean that I don't believe in the power of sharing your faith with people you've just met. I know people who have reached hundreds, even thousands of people for Christ by sharing their faith with strangers. I still do that today when the door is open to me. There are times when a few moments with a stranger is all you have. I often share my faith during an airplane flight or when I meet someone at a party or an event, after which I know I'll probably never see them again. There are many times in life when moments are all you have. And as believers, we should take advantage of every opportunity God puts in our path if people express an interest.

But when given the choice, I'd much rather spend time mentoring someone in the faith. I'd rather introduce them to Jesus the way he is most effectively introduced. And that takes time and patience and diligence. It takes a conscious decision to sow into the lives of others in order to reap a harvest of salvation.

Why Mentoring Works

I won't call this method of sharing your faith a divine revelation, because I'm certainly not the first person to come up with the idea. What I will call it is a comfortable fit.

I'm a very relational person by nature. And I have a naturally gregarious personality. When I walk down a busy street, I don't see a sea of strangers on the sidewalk; I see potential friends that I simply haven't had time to meet yet. I love people, and I love getting to know them better.

There's nothing I'd rather do than sit across the table from someone and find out about their life. I want to know what motivates them, what drives them, what moves them, what brings them to tears, what makes them laugh. I want to know where they're from, how they were raised, and what kind of parents they had. I love asking questions and finding out what people are thinking and feeling.[4]

I also enjoy sharing my own story and talking about the things that make me who I am. I like telling people about my childhood and what it was like driving my dog team as I was growing up in the backwoods of Alaska. And mostly, I love talking about Jesus and the wonderful things he's done in my life. In short, I enjoy developing close relationships with others. I enjoy getting to know them better and allowing them to get to know me.

And isn't that what mentoring is all about?

Obviously, not everyone has my extroverted personality. You may be more reserved or private in nature, but that shouldn't deter you from mentoring others. Mentoring is actually a very intimate process and doesn't require a gregarious personality. In fact, many of the best mentors I know are very introverted and quiet in a crowd. They tend to be extremely shy in group settings, but when it comes to visiting with a friend over coffee, just one-on-one, they become very comfortable and effective.

The reason I enjoy mentoring people to Jesus is that I can walk them through the process. I'm not trying to rush them into a decision for Christ. Instead, I'm allowing the truths of Scripture to simmer in their spirit. They can assimilate the words of Jesus at their own pace and don't feel pressured into praying a prayer of salvation before they're ready. It's a natural process, not a hurried or forced one.

Today I use this strategy of sharing Jesus on a daily basis. When someone comes to me with questions about Jesus or the Christian faith, I'm happy to answer. But immediately afterward, I say something like, "I'd love to really explore your questions with you and get to know you better. Why don't you and I get together next week and talk about this further? Just give me one hour of your time, and I'll do my best to answer your questions in more depth."

Then during our meeting, I don't waste any time getting to the point. I answer any questions they have and then suggest that we continue meeting one day a week for an hour each time. Almost everyone I've asked is willing to do that. And it's not because I'm particularly fun or articulate. It's because people respond to relationships. People long to be known and to be understood. It's how we are made. We are hardwired to connect with others, and we all long to have meaningful friendships with those around us.

Mentoring works because it meets the most basic and essential need within every one of us.

The Jesus Model

As we've already discussed, mentoring is also the method that Jesus modeled for us during his days on earth. When Jesus began his ministry, he didn't do it by announcing the start of a new church. He didn't set up a booth in the corner of a courtyard and begin preaching. And he didn't put together a handful of flyers to pass out on the street corner.

What Jesus did was handpick a few men to become his disciples. Men who would walk with him through the journey of life. Men who would watch him and learn from him as he went about his day. They would pray with him, eat with him, travel with him, and then sit with him by an open campfire at the end of the day. He lived his life in front of them, and they became like family to him. He allowed them to see firsthand how he handled stress and struggles, how he applied his faith to every circumstance, how he treated the people he met along the road. They saw him heal the sick, care for the poor, preach on the mountainsides, and confront the Pharisees and religious zealots.

They witnessed how he dealt with the everyday issues of life, like work and taxes and finances and difficult people. They walked with him through storms and sunny days, through times of trial and times of joy, through moments of suffering and pain and moments of happiness. They even watched him die.

And the mentoring process began with two simple words: "Follow me."

Jesus didn't bombard his disciples with information or hand them a three-hundred-page syllabus to memorize before morning. He didn't start his journey with a written test or a long form he needed them to fill out.

What Jesus asked for was a commitment of time. For the chance to sow into their lives and show them who he was and what he believed. He asked for the opportunity to earn their loyalty and respect.

This is the approach I use every day as I reach out to students at Stanford. Though I am still a very long way from being the kind of disciple I desire to be, hundreds of present and former Stanford athletes are now following Jesus because they have fallen in love with the Jesus they've seen in the Scriptures.

Mentoring is the method that Jesus modeled for us, and it's still the best method I know to reach the world for Christ. Just one person at a time. One meeting at a time. One week at a time.

4

The Power of the Gospel

The world has yet to see what God will do with and for and through and in and by the man who is fully consecrated to Him.

—D. L. Moody

Johnny was the most radical and disruptive person I had ever met. He was a Communist and a political revolutionary. And he was about as far from Jesus as a person can get. I met him while working at Reading University in England. And ours was the most unlikely friendship you could possibly imagine.

After the three-month training period at Berkeley ended, our training team traveled the United States in eight Volkswagen buses, stopping at universities and recruiting students to work with Campus Crusade. Then after another summer of training, Bud Hinkson divided our University Ambassador Team into two groups and took us to Europe. A smaller team went to Berlin, and the other went to different colleges and universities in the United Kingdom. I was assigned to begin building relationships with the students at Reading University, one of the more elite universities in England.

In the United Kingdom, students had to score in the top 2 percent of their class to be accepted into a university, so the students we dealt with were extremely bright and well educated. And they didn't think much of Americans. They were actually a pretty snobbish and arrogant group of people, and not very easy to reach. I thought kids at Berkeley were difficult, but they were nothing like the students we set out to share our faith with at Reading. It wasn't an easy assignment.

During my second year at Reading, some students who had made a commitment to follow Jesus challenged me by saying they knew one student I would never be able to reach for Christ. They told me his name was Johnny, and he spent almost all of his time in downtown London leading huge crowds in anti–Vietnam War demonstrations. He was the most visible Communist radical and antiestablishment organizer on campus.

I'm still not sure why I took my friends up on their challenge, but I asked for Johnny's off-campus address and shortly thereafter decided to pay him a visit.

I climbed the long stairway to his flat, found his apartment, took a deep breath, and knocked on the door. "Just a minute," I heard from inside, followed by a string of coughs and wheezes. A few seconds later he opened the door, covering his mouth with a Kleenex. He was a tall, good-looking kid, with disheveled hair and bags beneath his eyes, obviously fighting some kind of illness. I smiled and introduced myself, and he immediately invited me in.

The walls of his tiny apartment were plastered with posters of Che Guevara, the Argentine Communist revolutionary who had been trained in Cuba and then began wreaking havoc in Latin America. Though Johnny had English parents, he had been raised in Venezuela. He was apparently a chain-smoker, because the entire apartment reeked of cigarette smoke. He explained that he had been battling a bad case of bronchitis and then invited me to sit down.

"Can I make you a cup of instant coffee?" he asked with a huge smile.

"I'd love a cup," I answered, somewhat surprised by his cordial attitude, given that he had no idea who I was.

After a few minutes of small talk over really bad coffee, he finally asked me, "So what are you doing here in England?" It was his polite way of asking, "Why are you in my apartment and what do you want with me?"

"I'm here to talk to you about my close friend, the greatest revolutionary the world has ever known," I told him.

His eyes grew wide as saucers. "You know Che?" he said.

"No, Johnny, I'm here to talk about an even greater revolutionary. Jesus of Nazareth."

It wasn't the answer he expected. His neck stiffened and his entire demeanor changed. I fully expected him to rise from his chair and ask me to leave, but instead he began telling me about the exploits of Che Guevara and the great things he had accomplished in Latin America. I listened patiently and waited for an opportunity to change the subject back to Jesus.

For the next two hours, Johnny and I sat in his apartment exchanging ideas. I would tell him a story about the positive impact Jesus had had on the world, and he would immediately counter it with a story about Che Guevara. He went up one wall with his view of revolution, and I came down the other with mine. With our different backgrounds, there seemed to be no hope that we would ever see eye to eye.

Eventually I told him I had to leave, and he surprised me by saying, "This has been intriguing. I'd like to continue this discussion tomorrow."

I couldn't believe my ears. I thought I had been wasting my words, but apparently he wanted to hear more. So I agreed, and the next day we met again. This time I actually had the chance to share with him the message of how he could begin a relationship with Jesus. Though he continued to talk about Che, I could tell his heart was starting to open up.

Johnny was a dedicated activist, so I showed him the radical teachings of Jesus and the revolutionary ideas he brought into the world. Jesus' message of hope was a life-altering one, and he had a greater impact on humanity than any man who has ever lived. The more I told him about Jesus, the more intrigued Johnny became.

He and I continued to meet several times a week to study the teachings and claims of Jesus, until one day, when I sensed that his heart had softened, I asked him if he was ready to accept Jesus as his Lord and Savior. He said yes, and right there the two of us bowed our heads and I led him in prayer as he invited Jesus to come into his life. It might have been the most profoundly moving moment of my life.

A Radical Transformation

Johnny didn't just become a believer that day; he became the most radical spokesman for Jesus I had ever known. He took the phrase "on fire for the Lord" to an entirely new level. All of the passion and energy that he had been expending to promote Communist ideas were suddenly funneled into a desire to serve Jesus. And he began sharing what he was learning with his friends, most of whom were part of the antiestablishment movement—his radical, pro-Communist colleagues and allies.

Johnny was a charismatic spokesman, and he had a lot of credibility with this crowd, so many of them came to know the Lord. In just a few short weeks he had a huge impact for Jesus on that campus. It was an exciting thing to witness, and with each new believer his passion grew even greater.

Johnny and I became the best of friends during my stay in England. Because of his involvement in the anti-Vietnam rallies, he had not studied enough to pass his first-year exams the previous year, and he had only one more chance to pass them or he would never be allowed to get a degree from a British university. Knowing how much that degree meant to him, I did something I had never done before: I moved him into a spare bedroom in my home and told him to stop talking to people about Jesus until he had passed those exams. Each day I brought him the books he needed from the campus library. Thankfully, he was able to pass all of his courses.

After two more years, he graduated and joined the ministry of Campus Crusade for Christ in England. Eventually he went back to his home country of Venezuela and began a movement there among students. His work with young people ultimately morphed into a powerful ministry to homeless children living on garbage dumps.

When I think about how many lives have been impacted through Johnny's faith, I am humbled that God allowed me to play a small role in helping him come to faith. Countless people have been led to faith through his commitment to Jesus, and many more have been given food and shelter through his ministry. And to think that it all began with a simple conversation between friends. My new friends told me there was no way I could ever convince Johnny to follow Jesus, and I was just stubborn enough to take them up on that challenge. I'm so thankful I didn't back down.

My relationship with Johnny taught me never to discount anyone as a potential follower of Jesus. Often the people who appear to be the most hardened to hearing the Good News are the ones whose hearts are being prepared by the Holy Spirit to listen.

It's so tempting to take the path of least resistance. There are people in our lives who seem open to talking about Jesus, and those are the ones we focus on. We find a friend or neighbor who has been asking about our faith and appears eager to learn about Jesus, and we home in on them, looking for an opportunity to share with them. That's a good thing to do. But there are also people around us who seem hard and unreachable, and it's important not to overlook them. We never know who is ready to respond to God's call when it comes.

Some of the most powerful witnesses for Jesus have been the very people who most assumed would never be interested in hearing the message. And often the ones who seem the most distant from Jesus are the ones most open to discussing him. It's a dynamic I've seen time and again through the years.

I've learned to never underestimate what the Holy Spirit is doing in the hearts of those who seem far from God.

The Miracle at Pentecost

In the book of Acts, Luke records a miraculous event that happened on the day of Pentecost, a major Jewish feast. A group of believers was praying and worshiping when the Holy Spirit descended from heaven and filled the house where they were meeting with his glory. They all began speaking in other languages as the Spirit enabled them, and the sound drew a huge crowd from the city, each one coming to see what all the commotion was about. Scripture says the onlookers were "amazed and perplexed" and asked each other, "What does this mean?" (Acts 2:12).

Peter took the opportunity to share the gospel message with the crowd that had gathered: "Repent and be baptized, every one of you, in the name of Jesus Christ for the forgiveness of your sins. And you will receive the gift of the Holy Spirit. The promise is for you and your children and for all who are far off—for all whom the Lord our God will call" (2:38–39).

Three thousand people responded to Peter's invitation that day and accepted Jesus as their Lord and Savior. And from that day forward, "the Lord added to their number daily those who were being saved" (v. 47).

Almost every pastor I know has used this passage at one time or another to illustrate what God can do to draw people to himself through the power of the Holy Spirit. But the truth is most of us have never seen this kind of response to the message of Jesus. The story fascinates us, but it's pretty far outside of our own personal experiences.

Like those who gathered to see what the commotion was about, you and I are probably still "amazed and perplexed" by the story.

And perhaps that's why we struggle to believe that our efforts to reach out will have much impact on those who are seekers. Somewhere in the back of our minds, we doubt that the Holy Spirit will do the same miracle among our small group of friends and acquaintances.

I'll never forget the day God taught me to never again let those kinds of doubts enter my mind.

The Miracle at Villanova

It happened while I was still working with Campus Crusade in California, just a few weeks before we were scheduled to move to England. I got a call from a board member of Campus Crusade who lived near Villanova University, just outside of Philadelphia. He invited me to come and spend a few days with him before I had to depart for England. He had a heart for the athletes at Villanova and wanted me to break ground there, after which he would follow up with anyone who showed an interest.

At the time, I knew almost nothing about Villanova, except that their track team had recently won a national championship. I remembered reading an article about a runner named Dave who had actually beaten Jim Ryun in a track meet, setting a new world record in the process. Jim Ryun was the first high school student to ever break the four-minute mile and was at the peak of his college career at the time, so when Dave beat him, it quickly became a national news story.

When I got to Villanova, I hoped that I would have an opportunity to meet Dave, so I immediately began asking about him around campus. One student pointed me toward his dorm, so I took a chance at finding him at home and knocked on his door.

Amazingly enough, Dave answered the door and was polite enough to invite me in. We made small talk for a few minutes, and I told him I was visiting from California. After a few minutes he asked, "So what brings you to the Villanova campus?"

My initial thought was to say I was just visiting friends in Philadelphia and had read about him in the paper, so thought I would take the opportunity to try to meet him. That would have been the most reasonable answer. But something in me rose up and convicted me to be bold and straightforward. So I said to him, "I'm here talking to men about how they can have a personal relationship with God if they're interested. Are you interested?"

He stood still and stone-faced for several seconds. Then he responded, "This is unbelievable!" He shook his head in disbelief and then told me an amazing story. "Three weeks ago, right after I set the world record, I was euphoric. I had hoped the feeling would continue for the rest of my life, but it didn't last long. It actually left me feeling empty, so I began searching for God."

He went on to tell me how he had sought out people he respected on campus and began asking them about how to know God, but none of the answers they gave rang true to him. He went to three different friends, and each time the response they gave left him more confused and frustrated.

"Can you help me?" he asked.

I couldn't have been more thrilled. I smiled and pulled the *Four Spiritual Laws* booklet out of my back pocket, and the two of us sat across from each other in his room as I read through the principles that explained how he could begin a relationship with Jesus. Then I asked him if he'd like to pray and invite Jesus to come into his heart. "I really would," he answered. So the two of us bowed our heads as I led him in a prayer of salvation.

The minute he raised his head, his eyes were wide with excitement, and he said, "This is the greatest news I've ever heard! Every guy on my team needs to hear this! Would you come with me to the student union and talk to my friends about Jesus?"

His request was a first for me, so I wasn't sure what to say. But I also wasn't about to miss an opportunity to share Jesus with some other athletes. So I quickly agreed.

Dave took me to the campus student center and we found a quiet booth in the corner, then he said to me, "You wait here and I'm going to bring one of my friends to talk to you. After that, I'll bring a different guy every hour. I want all of my teammates to hear the story of Jesus!"

His exuberance was a little overwhelming, but I wasn't about to discourage him, so I assured him I'd talk to any friend interested in meeting with me. He hurried off and returned less than ten minutes later with one of his teammates. He introduced us, then said to his friend, "You need to hear what Jim has to say."

His friend sat down across from me, and once again I took out a *Four Spiritual Laws* booklet and began reading through it with him. I explained the message of salvation and then asked if he'd like to invite Jesus into his heart. "Yes, I would," he answered, so we bowed our heads and prayed together.

No sooner had we finished praying when Dave came walking up with another friend in tow. Once again he introduced us and said to his friend, "Jim has a story you need to hear. Why don't you sit down and talk with him?"

Again I began sharing the Good News. And just like before, this friend also asked me to pray with him when we finished. I couldn't believe how receptive they were to talking about Jesus and how ready they were to accept him as their Savior.

Over the next five days, I sat in that same booth in the corner of the student center every afternoon as Dave brought friends from his team to talk to me. As I recall, he brought twenty-six of his friends to talk with me in that time, and twenty-five of them accepted Jesus. It was the most exciting and miraculous week of my life.

I'm not vain enough to think that it was my eloquence or warm disposition that attracted people to the message. It was the Holy Spirit working to draw people to himself. I simply made myself available and followed God's lead as he softened the hearts of those he had been calling.

The apostle Paul wrote, "So neither the one who plants nor the one who waters is anything, but only God, who makes things grow. The one who plants and the one who waters have one purpose, and they will each be rewarded according to their own labor. For we are co-workers in God's service" (1 Cor. 3:7–9).

God is constantly working to draw people to himself, and you and I are simply the means through which he draws them. I've never taken any credit for the people I've helped lead to Christ, but it's always been a thrill to be part of God's process. When he draws men and women to himself, it's a beautiful thing to behold!

My Journey to Stanford

One of my greatest joys in life was getting to know Dr. Bill Bright, who founded Campus Crusade for Christ. One of the benefits of working with Campus Crusade as a young man was that I got to spend time with him. Much of what I know today about leading people to Jesus came directly from Dr. Bright and Bud Hinkson. Both have gone home to their eternal reward, but I cannot thank them enough for what they modeled for me. They were both friends and mentors.

My years in England at Reading University turned out to be a pivotal time in my life and career. Not only did I learn how to effectively share my faith with the most hardened skeptics, but I realized how much I enjoyed reaching out to athletes. God used my time there to bring my calling into clear focus. Campus Crusade had a division of their ministry called Athletes in Action, dedicated to reaching out to athletes, so that's where I decided to focus my time and energy.

After my time in England, Campus Crusade assigned me to work with Athletes in Action at the University of Mississippi, so I packed my bags and prepared to move to Oxford, Mississippi. But before starting my time there, Campus Crusade asked me to direct a week-long football conference in California. About a hundred athletes would be converging on Southern California in order to get into shape physically and spiritually, and I was asked to oversee the event.

I was assigned a room with three athletes attending the conference, two of whom had just completed their freshman year at Stanford University. They also both had been led to the Lord recently.

One of them was a young man named Jeff Siemon, who would later go on to become a consensus All-American athlete and a first-round draft pick after his senior year. He was recently inducted into the College Football Hall of Fame. The other was a man named Dennis Sheehan, who today is one of the leading cardiologists in the country.

Since both of these men were new believers, they had a lot of questions about their faith, so we spent long hours in the room studying and discussing the questions they had. I got to know them really well during the conference, and one day they told me how much they wished I could come back to Stanford with them. "There are lots of athletes on the team that really need answers," they told me. "God could use you there to help reach out to them."

I'd love to have taken them up on their offer, but I had already been assigned to the Ole Miss campus. "Maybe someday that will happen," I told them.

I never forgot that conversation, and after a year of working with student athletes in Mississippi, I asked Athletes in Action to transfer me to Stanford. So in the fall of 1970, I packed my bags for

Stanford, and I've never looked back. The minute I stepped onto the Stanford campus, something told me I was exactly where God wanted me to be. And the last forty-plus years have proven that feeling to be right on target.

It's been an incredible journey!

Changing the World

When recruiting young people to work with the Campus Crusade ministry, Dr. Bright would always say to them, "Come help change the world." That phrase quickly became the motto for Campus Crusade.

Dr. Bright understood the contagious nature of the Good News and the powerful effect that the Holy Spirit can have on the world when we choose to walk in obedience to God. He knew that even the smallest spark could engulf the world's largest forest. He recognized that we were doing far more than sharing the Good News about Jesus; we were on a mission to change the world.

That's a philosophy that I take with me every day to the Stanford campus as I mentor students in their faith. I never want to discount what God is capable of doing in the hearts and lives of young men and women. And I never want to second-guess which ones God has been working to draw to himself and what great things he has in store for their future.

Every time I pray with a new believer, I silently wonder if this young man will grow to be the next Billy Graham or Josh McDowell or Bud Hinkson. Or Dr. Bill Bright. Every time I open my Bible to study with a new believer, I wonder what God will accomplish through my feeble efforts and what vision he has for their life. And I pray that he will give me the right words to say and the right thoughts to implant in order to help them catch and carry out that vision.

As I sit at my small table in the Stanford Sports Café day after day, looking out over a sea of students bustling to and from their classes, I don't see a herd of bright-eyed college kids away from home for the first time. And I don't see a bunch of spoiled and apathetic kids looking for a good time. Those stereotypes never enter my mind.

What I see are talented and eager young men and women looking for something to give their lives meaning. I see an ocean of untapped resources just waiting to be used for God's glory. I see thousands of books waiting to be written; mountains of clay waiting to be shaped and molded into something beautiful; acres of acorns in a dry field, each struggling to take root and grow into a mighty oak tree.

I see people created in the image of God, lost and orphaned children, each seeking to find their way home. I see individuals in need of a Savior. And I know that God has put me on the Stanford campus for all these years to help them find what they're looking for.

You and I have been entrusted with a great treasure, and we should never allow ourselves to keep that treasure hidden.

Pray today that God would lead you to the person in your life whom the Holy Spirit has been preparing to accept his call of salvation. Allow yourself to be used by God as he works to draw all men and women to himself.

Come help God change the world.

5

Effective Principles of Mentoring: Part 1

Just as a nursing mother cares for her children, so we cared for you.

—1 Thessalonians 2:7–8

Many years ago someone recommended to me a book titled *The Master Plan of Evangelism* by Robert E. Coleman. It's a small book, barely 120 pages long, but it has done more to shape my view of how to share my faith through mentoring than any book I've read—besides the Bible, of course.

It's a fascinating book that outlines eight principles of mentoring that Coleman gleaned from the life and teachings of Jesus. I encourage anyone interested in mentoring others to pick up a copy to read.

Through the years, I've developed my own unique principles of mentoring, and I believe they are the key reason our Sports Challenge ministry has been so successful in reaching and mentoring so many student athletes at Stanford. Everything I do is guided by these simple but effective principles of mentoring.

Let's take some time to explore these principles in greater detail. Whether the Lord has called you to mentor two friends or twenty, these timeless principles should prove invaluable to the process.

Principle #1: *Choosing Well*

The first and most obvious step in mentoring others is choosing the people God would have you mentor. This is actually the most critical step in the process, since we all have only so many hours in the day. You and I are not called to mentor every person who comes across our path, so it's important to be selective and allow God to guide the process.

Most of the students I mentor are not believers when we first begin to meet. The majority of them have been referred to me by a teammate or a friend. I never turn down an opportunity to share Jesus with another person, but I also don't assume that every person I share with will become a long-time mentoree. I simply follow God's lead and trust him to make that decision.

After getting to know the student for a couple of weeks, I explain to them that there are some basic things I go through with each student who sits down across from me. First, we spend time reading through the booklet *Would You Like to Know God Personally?*, which is an updated version of the *Four Spiritual Laws* booklet I used for so many years.[5] It explains clearly how a person can begin a relationship with Jesus.

I am convinced that a relationship with Jesus is where life truly begins, so I explain to them that at some point in their life they will probably want to begin this relationship, and I want them to know how to do it when they feel the time is right. I never pressure anyone.

After our initial meeting, if they indicate a desire to continue, we begin meeting each week for an hour to examine the life and claims of Jesus. Almost every student who continues meeting with me eventually begins a relationship with Jesus. The gospel is a compelling message, and very few will reject Jesus when they're able to see who he truly is and the life of salvation that he offers to those who accept him.

Once a student accepts Jesus into their life, the mentoring process takes on a new dynamic. That's when I begin the work of helping them get to know him better. They are no longer a seeker of the truth; they are a budding disciple of Jesus under my care and guidance. I attempt to help them move from newborn status to pursuing a process of maturing in their faith. And I don't take that responsibility lightly.

Just as Jesus modeled a level of intentionality with the disciples he mentored, I try to model that same type of intentional relationship with my mentorees.

The twelve disciples Jesus selected were handpicked among hundreds of followers and set apart for the specific purpose of teaching and mentoring. What we often forget, though, is that for every disciple he chose, there were many followers who didn't get chosen. I'm certain Jesus was aware of this fact, but he understood his mission and he stuck to it. He likely left some wondering why they didn't get picked and may have even hurt some feelings in the process.

Scripture tells us he arrived at his decision after a night of prayer (Luke 6:12–13), so there was no doubt which twelve he should choose. Every decision Jesus made was perfectly aligned with God's will, so we know the twelve he picked were a perfect choice.

I've never pretended to be perfect, and I'm certainly not as tuned in to God's will as Jesus, so I have to take a slightly different approach. Like Jesus, I always spend a great deal of time in prayer, seeking God's guidance when choosing which men I should mentor. And I pick the men that I feel God has specifically put in my path who express a desire to follow Jesus. Sometimes God makes his choice glaringly obvious, and other times I have to take a leap of faith, but I always seek God's will before taking on a student to mentor.

I'm also not as good at discipling as Jesus, so instead of twelve, my inner circle consists of thirty to thirty-five men at a time. And each of these men agrees to meet with me for at least one hour a week for an intentional time of spiritual and life coaching as we dig into the Scriptures.

Obviously, very few people will be able to devote this much time to mentoring others. I'm able to do this because mentoring is my full-time career. You may have only a few hours a week or an hour a day to meet with others. I encourage you to pray and diligently seek God before overextending yourself.

Many years ago I decided to focus my time and energies on mentoring student athletes. I knew I needed to choose wisely which segment of the student body would allow me to have the greatest impact, so I decided to center my energies on students within the Stanford athletic department.

I've always been a good athlete, and I played every sport I could fit into my schedule as a kid. As a young boy I was mostly obsessed with football and baseball. When I wasn't playing sports I was out fishing or hunting. Though I enjoy times of solitude, I've always been happier and more productive when I'm staying active.

God also chose to gift me with exceptionally good hand-eye coordination, which allowed me to become a table tennis champion while I was in college. This God-given talent has opened many doors to share with athletes and coaches who respect my accomplishments.

Athletes tend to respond well to other athletes, so focusing my ministry on the Stanford sports teams felt like an obvious decision. I relate to athletes and they seem to relate well to me, and our love of sports is something we have in common. This is where I choose to build relationships because this is where I feel God can most use me.

You may have other interests. Perhaps your passion is riding motorcycles or deep-sea diving or fly-fishing. Whatever your interests, you likely have friends and acquaintances who share those interests, and that could be your greatest sphere of influence.

Selecting well is an important first step when seeking to mentor your friends to Jesus. God doesn't call us to reach out to every person with whom we come into contact. But he does call us to use the gifts and influences we have to the best of our abilities. God is always putting people he wants us to reach in our path, and too often we miss the opportunity simply because we aren't paying attention or we're preoccupied with the daily chores of life.

I encourage you to spend time praying about where God wants to use you and which people he has placed in your path. If you feel him leading you to focus on a select group of people, or even one specific person, pray that he will guide you as you commit to following his lead.

We are all called to be ministers of the Good News and to share Christ with our friends. But how we go about doing that should be a prayerful and intentional decision.

Principle #2: *Investing in the Relationship*

Whenever I take on a new student to mentor, there are a number of things I go over on our first meeting. I want to make sure they understand what they are signing up for when they agree to meet with me each week.

One of the things I tell them is that I intend to become one of their best friends, and I want them to see me as someone they can trust implicitly. Nothing they say will ever be repeated, and I'll never judge them for any actions or struggles they choose to share with me.

I also let them know that I am available twenty-four hours a day if they need me, and they should never hesitate to call if they need to talk. Obviously, I encourage them to respect the fact that I'm married, so I won't be available to chat about the weather at 2:00 a.m., but in the midst of a crisis I'm always there for them, no matter what time of day or night it happens to be. I want to be the first person who comes to mind when they need prayer or guidance or simply a shoulder to cry on.

I tell them that nothing they want to talk about is off-limits, whether it's grades or girls or parents or struggles with their sports. I encourage them to open their life up to me, and I, in turn, will do the same.

I tell them if they have a spiritual question, I'll do my best to answer it. And if I don't have the answer, we'll explore the Scriptures together. I never pretend to be something I'm not or smarter than I am.

But perhaps the most important thing I tell them is that I am fully committed to our relationship. I let them know that I see our mentoring relationship as much more than a weekly Bible study or a teacher relaying advice to his student. Our mentoring partnership is to become a sacred and nonnegotiable bond. It is a two-way commitment that I take very seriously, and one that I expect them to honor as well.

I see the weekly meetings I have with my mentorees as simply a starting point for a much deeper and more meaningful friendship. And I do all I can to prove that to the students I mentor. I find out when they have games, and I show up on the sidelines to cheer them on. When their parents come for a visit, I make it a point to meet them. When they have a big test or final coming up, I call to make sure they're spending time studying and preparing. When they have a date, I remind them of their commitment to purity, and afterward I ask if they stayed true to that commitment.

The association I have with those I mentor is far more than a passing friendship and much more involved than a teaching role. I become an integral part of their world, and they become an integral part of mine.

This is how Jesus taught his disciples, and it's the best approach that I know for growing godly men and women in the kingdom.

Principle #3: *Teaching Spiritual Obedience*

Jesus expected his disciples to obey his commandments, and I expect the same of my mentorees. Not to obey me, mind you, but to obey the commandments of Jesus.

A consecrated life is the bellwether of a true follower of Jesus and should be the primary pursuit of any true believer. Of course, this is a maturation process. I did not expect my three children to act and reason as adults when they were still in diapers. Neither do I expect spiritually mature perspectives and actions from a newborn believer.

Godly living is critical to every Christian walk, and it's one of the most important facets of a mentoring relationship.

In my particular ministry, this is a truth I deal with on a daily basis. Today's college students face tremendous temptation to get involved in activities that don't reflect the character of Jesus. Most are away from home for the very first time and enjoying a level of freedom that they've never before experienced. The pressure to give in to the temptations of lust and drinking and drugs and other immoral behaviors can be overwhelming. I'm not sure there is any period of life that brings greater opportunity for moral failures and poor life choices than the college years. Often these poor choices leave damaging scars.

That's why a huge part of my mentoring is devoted to teaching students how to live godly lives according to the Scriptures and encouraging them to remain true to their commitment to Jesus. I don't judge them, because we all struggle with temptation. I simply love them where they are while challenging them to become the kind of men that God wants them to be.

Peter wrote, "His divine power has given us everything we need for a godly life through our knowledge of him who called us by his own glory and goodness" (2 Pet. 1:3).

Through the indwelling of the Holy Spirit, you and I have been given the power to overcome sin and live a life of integrity and godliness. We have the power to consecrate ourselves to God's will and overcome the temptations that Satan brings into our path. I want the students I mentor to understand their commitment to God and embrace the power that God has given them to overcome these challenges!

Principle #4: *Passing It On*

Another important element to being a follower of Christ is learning to pass on to others what Jesus has given to us. Sharing the Good News with others is just a small part of our responsibility as believers. We're also expected to pass on whatever knowledge or wisdom the Holy Spirit has imparted to us.

Paul described his life in Christ as being "poured out like a drink offering" (2 Tim. 4:6). Paul had spent much of his adult life serving God, and because of that he had years of godly insight and understanding that younger believers didn't have. He understood his responsibility as a seasoned believer to sow into the lives of others.

In a lot of ways, mentoring is like being an experienced gardener. A gardener not only sows the seeds but also tends his plants daily in order to help them grow. He gives his garden just the right amounts of water and sunshine and weeding at the right times and places. He works the soil, keeping it fresh and fertile and productive, making sure it has all the nutrients it needs to grow.

Just like an experienced gardener, a mentor keeps a sharp eye on those he is mentoring, using his skills and knowledge to help them grow strong and healthy in their faith. And when the time comes, he reaps a harvest of righteousness and eternal fruit.

My father is a good example of this principle. For many years he modeled great faithfulness among the native people of Alaska with seemingly little in the way of results. But he stayed the course. He kept loving and serving and caring for the people of our small community, tirelessly spreading God's message of hope.

Eventually his faithfulness bore fruit. The blessings of his work began to flow through our community, and many who had observed him for years started coming to Jesus. The ripple effect of his faithful service was an amazing thing to witness.

After he and Mom had gone home to be with the Lord, the legislature of Alaska voted unanimously to honor them with a citation of excellence and thanks for all they had done for the native people of Alaska. From what I was told, it was the first unanimous vote in the history of the state legislature. It was a huge honor to our family and a testament to my parents' great faith in God.

My dad's favorite verse was Psalm 126:6: "They weep as they go to plant their seed, but they sing as they return with the harvest" (NLT).

Even when we can't see the results of our faithfulness, God wants us to keep planting. To keep sowing into the lives of others. To impart the love and wisdom that he has imparted to us. And then he takes our small acts of obedience and turns them into a bountiful crop of righteousness for the kingdom.

6

Effective Principles of Mentoring: Part 2

And the things you have heard me say in the presence of many witnesses entrust to reliable people who will also be qualified to teach others.

—2 Timothy 2:2

When I was a young believer, Bud Hinkson became my primary mentor, and he set out to teach me everything he knew about walking consistently with Jesus and learning to share my faith in a way that makes sense. He had a lot of spiritual "gray hair" that I simply didn't have, so I attached myself to him. He not only taught me how to live a Christlike life; he modeled for me what that looks like. I am forever indebted to Bud and his wife, Shirley, for the things I learned from them.

Today I am a seasoned believer, and I spend my days pouring out my life for those who look to me for guidance. When I mentor a young man in his faith, I call on all the experiences I've gained through the years to try to teach and mold him into the man God wants him to be. I make no claims of being perfect—I've made my share of bad decisions. But I do have enough spiritual insight and knowledge to say to others, "Watch me and do as I do, as I follow Jesus."

Principle #5: *Modeling Your Faith*

One of the most important aspects of being an effective mentor is learning to model the faith and character you are trying to teach. That's why this principle is so critical to being a successful spiritual mentor.

It's my job as a mentor to model the Christian faith as well as teach it. My desire is to help others develop a deeper and more meaningful relationship with Jesus simply by allowing them to come alongside me as I seek to draw nearer to God in my own walk.

A few years ago, I decided to form a small student leadership team on campus and invited a few of my more spiritually mature mentorees to join it. We called our group the Student Athlete Leadership Team (SALT). My intent was to handpick a group of student athletes that I felt were ready to begin mentoring other students on campus, and then focus our time together on training them to become spiritual mentors.

One of the first students I approached was a Stanford baseball player named Danny Putnam—a young man who later went on to have a successful career with the Oakland A's. Danny was an impressive young man with tremendous leadership skills, so he was an obvious choice.

One day Danny came to me with a great idea. He wanted to put together a written statement of faith—something like a Christian manifesto—outlining what it looks like to be an obedient follower of Christ. His intent was to create a document that articulated the purpose of our leadership team and also outlined some specific guidelines for any present or future students interested in joining.

Obviously, I was thrilled with the idea, so he and a few other members of our leadership team began working on it. Before long, they had produced a brilliant document they titled "The Call to Servant Leadership." It began with a passage from the book of Timothy:

> Don't let anyone look down on you because you are young, but set an example for the believers in speech, in conduct, in love, in faith and in purity. Watch your life and doctrine closely. . . . Persevere in them, because if you do, you will save both yourself and your hearers. (1 Tim. 4:12, 16)

The document went on to outline five specific areas of the Christian faith in which believers are expected to live exemplary lives in order to be effective ambassadors for Christ: in speech, in conduct, in love, in faith, and in purity.

Each of the five areas was outlined and expanded on in great detail, with specific examples of what godly character looks like. I was surprised by how thorough and detailed the students had been in putting the document together.

Once I approved the document, it was typed up and distributed to every member of the group, and each man was expected to sign it as a symbol of his commitment to living—and modeling—a Christlike life. Any future members of the leadership team were also expected to read and sign it before becoming part of the group.

The greatest thing about this document—besides the fact that it was the students who took the initiative to draft it—is that it perfectly articulates why it's important for believers to live pure and admirable lives. Obviously, it's because we are called to be obedient to God's Word, but it's also because people are watching us. The moment we give our lives to Jesus, we become ambassadors of Jesus on earth. And that's a responsibility we should never take lightly.

It's my job as a mentor to teach Christian principles to my students. But it's how I live that will have the greatest impact on their lives.

Faith is infectious. Just like every other aspect of the Christian life.

Principle #6: *Learning to Delegate Wisely*

Jesus made very few demands on his disciples for the first year or so that they were together. In Scripture we see them following Jesus and watching him as he healed and ministered and taught, but they didn't do much else. Often he would call on them to arrange for meals and accommodations for the group, but beyond that, they were expected to simply follow and observe.

It wasn't until their third trip to Galilee, which was almost two years into Jesus' ministry, that he began calling on them to put into practice the things they had learned. Mark records, "Calling the Twelve to him, he began to send them out two by two and gave them authority over impure spirits" (Mark 6:7).

This is the first time in Scripture that we see Jesus actually delegating a meaningful task to his disciples. And before they went, he gave them specific instructions about what to do and where to go, and even what to bring with them (see Mark 6:8–11).

Jesus wasn't being overly cautious. He just understood the patience it takes to teach people a new way of thinking and acting and reacting. He understood the importance of letting people learn at their own pace and then recognizing when they're ready to be pushed to the next level.

The athletes I mentor are bright young men, and they usually catch on to things very quickly. Many of them are more mature and disciplined than their peers, simply because they've had to work hard in order to excel at sports. By the time they come to Stanford, they've already developed a keen mind and a stellar work ethic. So there's a temptation for me to expect more from them than I might other students. But I resist that urge. I've learned the importance of being patient and intentional with them. I don't want to send them out before they're ready.

Today's college athletes are under tremendous pressure to succeed, and because of their high-profile status on campus, a lot of people tend to put undue demands on their time. At Stanford, though not as much as at "football factory" schools, athletes are often revered and respected more than many of them deserve, simply because they are athletes. Everyone wants to be friends with them. They're invited to all the parties and given first-class treatment wherever they go. It is no wonder so many pro athletes are such narcissists. They're often so idolized during the college years that they lose all sense of grounding and humility.

Because I work so closely with college athletes, I see this dynamic on a daily basis. Many of the young men I mentor are like campus celebrities, and once the word gets out that they have given their lives to Jesus, they feel even more pressure from the many Christian groups on campus. Churches and ministries are excited to learn about their newfound faith, and the invitations to speak about their spiritual journey begin flooding in—often within just a few weeks of their beginning this new relationship.

Many of these guys look to me for guidance as they navigate these unfamiliar waters. And my advice is almost always to take things slowly and manageably. I encourage them to pace themselves and even learn to say no when they don't feel ready. It's always a good idea to have a little spiritual maturity under your belt before giving the keynote address at a pastors' conference.

A mother eagle has to learn when it's time to push her eaglets out of the nest to find their wings. If she pushes them too soon, they might not survive the fall.

Principle #7: *Keeping a Watchful Eye*

Soon after the disciples were sent out on their first mission, they returned and gave Jesus an account of their successful journey. Mark records, "The apostles gathered around Jesus and reported to him all they had done and taught" (Mark 6:30).

Scripture doesn't record Jesus' response, but I think it's a good bet that he was proud of his young protégés. It's always an exciting thing as a spiritual mentor to see your students grow and excel in their faith. This is when the mentoring process really gets fun. When you see your mentorees spreading their wings and acting on what they've learned, you know that your hands-on work is almost done.

One of the greatest things about mentoring new believers is that they're so excited about their faith. Often as soon as they make a commitment to follow Jesus, the first thing they want to do is go out and share Jesus with others. I never discourage young Christians from doing this, and I love it when they come to our meetings with stories of conversations they've had with their friends. They often give me a blow-by-blow reenactment. I love seeing young people on fire for the Lord!

One of my primary roles as a mentor is to help keep this fire burning strong. I want my mentorees to remember the joy they felt when they first began their relationship with Jesus and to keep reexperiencing that joy. My desire is that their faith stays fresh and alive and exuberant. And one of the best ways to help it along is through continued supervision.

Too often believers experience a high at their spiritual birth, but soon the fire dwindles. Instead of burning hotter, they burn out and lose their zeal. That usually happens when they don't have anyone walking alongside them as they navigate the ups and downs of their newfound faith.

This is why supervision is such a critical role in the mentoring process. When people are left to go it alone, too often they end up going downhill.

I encourage the students I mentor to share with me all the highs and lows of their spiritual lives. I ask tough questions about the temptations they are going through and how they are overcoming them. I encourage them to stay in the Word and set aside time to spend alone with the Lord. I encourage them to attend church and get involved in their church body so they can get to know other believers of different ages, from various backgrounds, and with different occupations and interests.

In short, I encourage them to be doing all the things that every believer needs to be doing in order to grow in their faith. I love them through the stumbles and twists and turns that everyone faces. I am realistic, and I understand how quickly an untended faith can drift and dwindle.

Principle #8: *Training Mentorees to Mentor*

The ultimate goal of mentoring people in their faith is to prepare them to someday begin mentoring others in the faith. Without that, there really is little point in mentoring. Our charge is to "make disciples of all nations" (Matt. 28:19), and for that to happen, there needs to be a compound effect.

Several years ago I was invited to a prayer breakfast in Washington, and during the event my wife and I had the opportunity to meet a well-known businessman who had been extremely influential in funding outreach programs to Africa and other third world countries. I had heard a lot of stories about this man and was excited to get the chance to meet him.

He happened to glance down at the huge ring I was wearing. It was a National Championship tennis ring that had been presented to me by the Stanford tennis team captain—a man I had mentored.

"You must be from Stanford!" he said.

I explained that I didn't actually work for Stanford but served as a mentor to many of the athletes on campus. Then he asked, "Do you know Jeff Siemon?"

"Yes, I do," I answered. "In fact, I was his mentor when he attended Stanford."

His voice lifted with excitement. "Well, I need to tell you a story," he said. He told me that several years earlier, before he had become a believer, he got an invitation to attend a six-week intensive Bible study at Jeff's house. "I had no interest in studying the Bible, but Jeff had been my hero since I was a kid, so I'd have done anything to meet him. Even if it meant I had to study the Bible."

During the study, he and Jeff became close friends. He had always had a lot of uncertainties about the Bible and the validity of Scripture, and he continued bombarding Jeff with questions of apologetics, but each time Jeff patiently took time to talk it through. "No matter what question I asked, he always seemed to have an answer," he said.

On the last day of the program, he cornered Jeff in the main room of his house and told him, "You've answered every question I've ever had about the Bible, and I can no longer deny its authenticity. But I'm not sure what to do next."

Jeff said to him, "Now it's time to pray and ask Jesus to become your Lord and Savior." So the two of them bowed their heads as he asked Jesus into his life.

When he finished telling me the story, he said with a smile, "So you're the one who taught Jeff all that stuff about the Bible? I guess that makes you my spiritual grandfather!"

"I guess it does," I told him.

I can't remember the last time I had felt so honored.

The apostle Paul wrote to Timothy, "And the things you have heard me say in the presence of many witnesses entrust to reliable people who will also be qualified to teach others" (2 Tim. 2:2). Mentoring is a process of multiplication, and its effects pass down from generation to generation.

While gathering thoughts and stories for this book, I found myself making notes and lists of all the people I've had the privilege of working with during my life. I had to go deep into my memory banks to recall many of the names and faces of those I've had the opportunity to mentor.

What struck me most was just how many of the people I've been able to introduce to Jesus have gone on to be powerful forces for God's kingdom. As I look over the list, I see names of high-profile sports figures, politicians, pastors, missionaries, successful businessmen, motivational speakers, leaders of industry, and even some well-known celebrities and TV personalities. Many of the names you would recognize if I were to take the space to list them.

With very few exceptions, these people today are living out their faith in the place God has planted them. Many have had an enormous impact for Jesus on the world. And today, some of the young people I mentor are the children of those I helped lead to the Lord many years ago.

It is profoundly humbling to see what God has been able to accomplish through my meager efforts. As I sit at my tiny "office" in the Sports Café day after day, counseling young people and mentoring them in their walk with God, my efforts often feel so small and insignificant in the grand scheme of things. And there are days when I wonder if I'm making any kind of difference at all.

But then I look at what God has done with my modest efforts, and I realize that in his economy, no time spent reaching out to others is wasted. In God's hands, even the smallest act of obedience can have an impact that rings well into eternity.

WWJD

Most of us remember the "What Would Jesus Do?" movement that swept the country a few years ago. Many students at Stanford came to school wearing a WWJD bracelet. For many of them, it became a way of identifying themselves as followers of Jesus. I actually liked the trend, and I think it created a lot of opportunities for believers to discuss their faith with friends. It also served as a good reminder for believers to ask themselves in every situation, "What would Jesus do?"

I'm not much on bumper-sticker faith, but this particular question is a good one for all of us. And it begs even deeper questions.

If Jesus were in your shoes today—networking with your circle of friends and acquaintances, working at your job, living in your neighborhood, shopping at your local grocery store, sitting in the stands during your child's soccer games, eating lunch at your favorite restaurant—how would he go about having an impact on the world around him? What would Jesus do if he were in your shoes?

More important, how would Jesus bring your friends to faith?

In the next section, let's take some time to explore those questions further.

How Would Jesus
Bring Your Friends to Faith?

If you had the cure to cancer, wouldn't you share it? You have the cure to death . . . get out there and share it.

—Kirk Cameron

As I have loved you, so you must love one another.

—John 13:34

Whoever claims to live in him must live as Jesus did.

—1 John 2:6

7

He Would Accept Them as They Are

In order to establish trust with people we must love them with the baggage they bring with them.

—Rebecca Manley Pippert

Ralph was about as hostile and unlovable as any person I'd ever met. And he reeked of body odor. I literally had to hold my breath when I walked into his room.

I met Ralph during my time with Campus Crusade in England. A couple of the guys I had helped lead to the Lord told me about him during one of our weekly Bible studies. They said he was one of the brightest students at Reading University and was well known for disliking both Americans and Christians. Since I was both, they warned me not to waste my time trying to reach out to him.

Of course, that's all I needed to hear. I asked them for his address and that evening showed up outside his dorm room. He didn't answer the door when I knocked, just hollered "Who is it?" from inside his room.

"My name is Jim Stump, and I'd like to visit for a few minutes," I answered.

He must have recognized my name, because he immediately began cursing and shouting. "I know who you are," he barked. "You're that Christian guy from America who has come over here to convert all us heathens. I don't have time to talk to you. And I don't need saving, so just go away!"

"I promise not to stay long," I persisted. "I just wanted to come by and meet you. Just give me a few minutes of your time and then I'll be out of your way."

He cursed again and cracked open the door, then stuck his head around the edge to glare at me. "I'll give you five minutes," he said, "but it won't do you any good."

"Thanks, Ralph," I answered. "I promise I won't be long."

He shook his head and grunted before swinging the door open. "You've got five minutes, but then I want you out of here!"

I literally thought I would pass out when I walked into the room. The smell was unbearable, and the room was dirty and unkempt. Ralph didn't look any better. His hair was long and greasy, and his scraggly beard looked like a crow's nest. I hoped that the look on my face would not reflect what I was thinking as I made my way into the center of the room. He sat down in an old recliner, so I made my way to a couch across from him. I had to move dirty blankets and clothes out of the way before I could sit down.

Ralph reflected everything that traditionally turned me off in a person. He was rude and vulgar and unwashed, and he seemed to have no sense of respect for others. He was an angry and bitter person, and I found myself wondering why I was even there. I couldn't imagine someone like Ralph wanting to come to Christ, and I was likely just wasting my time.

He sat silently in his chair, glaring at me with a faraway look in his eyes. I had no idea how to begin or what I could possibly say to get through to him. *Dear God*, I prayed, *I know you love Ralph, but I do not even like him right now. If you want him to feel loved, you're going to have to love him. I'm incapable of doing that right now, but I am willing to be available to let you do it through me. I know you led me here for a reason. Help me, Lord.*

Incredibly my whole attitude changed, and I began to ask Ralph about his life. I asked about his family and his background. I asked where he was from, what had brought him to Reading University, and what he'd been studying. I asked about his friends and his interests. And then I sat back and listened.

At first he seemed reserved and reticent, like he didn't trust me, but the longer he talked, the more he opened up. Before long he was telling me details of his life. I was surprised by his transparency.

As I sat listening to Ralph tell me about his life and the pain he had experienced, a wave of compassion began welling up in my spirit. As my attitude began to change, the ambivalent feelings I had felt for him began to melt away, and I actually found myself enjoying our conversation. I began to care deeply about him.

He was nothing like the angry brute I had originally thought him to be.

Sunday Surprise

I lost track of time as I sat visiting with Ralph. At one point I realized that I hadn't yet begun sharing the Good News with him, so I took the *Four Spiritual Laws* booklet out of my back pocket and asked if he'd ever heard the story of Jesus. Just then his demeanor changed. He looked at his watch and said, "I told you five minutes and you've been here for forty-five minutes. I think it's time for you to leave." He rose from his chair and quickly escorted me to the door.

"I'm sorry I stayed so long," I said. "But can I leave you some material to read through?"

I gave him the *Four Spiritual Laws* booklet along with some other materials I had with me. He laid them on an end table without even looking at them, so I assumed he'd throw them away as soon as I left. I thanked him for his time and said, "I really enjoyed meeting you. I hope we get to visit again sometime." We shook hands and I went on my way, wondering if I had really done any good.

The next Sunday morning I got dressed for church and started out on the long, arduous walk to the building. It was a grueling trek each week, uphill most of the way, and always left me winded. Just as I reached the steps in front of the entrance, I was shocked to see Ralph leaning against the front rail. He was grinning from ear to ear.

"I'll bet you didn't expect to see me here, did you?" he said.

"Not really," I answered. "But I'm glad you're here."

He told me that after I had left his apartment a few nights earlier, he started to read through the material I gave him, and it made a huge impact on him. "I had never heard the story of Jesus before," he said, "and it really made me think." He read the booklet several times, and late that evening he prayed and asked Jesus to come into his heart. "I knew you went to church here, so I wanted to surprise you," he said with a Cheshire-cat grin.

I was so excited to hear the news that I gave him a big bear hug. He wrapped his arms around my neck and squeezed as though he would not let go.

"That is so great to hear," I told him several times. "I've been praying for you all week."

We talked for a few minutes before the service, and then just before going into the building he said to me, "You know, no one has ever shown me the kind of love and kindness that you did. Thanks for being my friend."

At that moment I realized just how profoundly the Lord had answered my prayer. I knew that it wasn't me showing love to Ralph that evening in his apartment; it was the Holy Spirit loving him through me. I could take no credit for it. But God loved Ralph deeply, and that was the love he felt. I was simply the conduit through which it was demonstrated.

Ralph and I went on to become good friends during my time at Reading. We began meeting each week to pray and study the Bible, and I watched him grow strong in his faith. He became one of my most dedicated students and quickly began witnessing to his friends, bringing a number of them to the Lord.

Today Ralph is a pastor who has planted a number of churches throughout the United Kingdom. Every summer he takes a trip to India and spends his time there mentoring local pastors, teaching them how to share the gospel and shepherd their flocks. He and I still stay in touch, and it's exciting to see the great things God has accomplished through him.

I am deeply grateful for the friendship I've been able to build with Ralph through the years. And I'm even more grateful that God used me in some small way to reach out to him. The experience of learning to love someone by faith has taught me more about reaching others for Jesus than a library full of books on evangelism.

The Woman at the Well

The apostle John records the story of a day that Jesus was traveling through Samaria. He came to a town called Sychar, which is near the land that Jacob had given to his son Joseph. Jacob's well was still there, being used by the people of the town for water.

The word *Sychar* means "town of drunkards." And the town lived up to its name. It was a wicked place filled with evil and debauchery. It was the antithesis of everything Jesus stood for, yet he chose to go through there on his travels.

Jesus sent his disciples into town to buy food while he rested beside Jacob's well. It was noon, and while he was there a lone Samaritan woman came to draw water from the well. Jesus struck up a conversation with her. "Will you give me a drink?" he asked (John 4:7).

Just talking to the woman was a scandalous act. Jewish customs forbade Jews from talking with Samaritans, and especially Samaritan women. And taking a drink from her cup would have deemed him ceremonially unclean. Even the woman was shocked by his request.

But Jesus didn't see her as an unclean Samaritan. He saw her as a woman who had been used and mistreated by every man she'd ever known. She felt both unloved and unlovable. The fact that she was drawing water at noon, during the hottest part of the day, indicated that she was trying to hide from the other women of the village and had likely suffered years of shame and scorn for her immoral lifestyle. She didn't have to be reminded of her sin; she lived with it every day of her life.

Even Jesus' disciples gasped when they saw him talking to a sinful Samaritan woman. But Jesus wasn't there to condemn her. He was there to bring hope of a brighter future and a better way to live. He told her, "Everyone who drinks this water will be thirsty again, but whoever drinks the water I give them will never thirst. Indeed, the water I give them will become in them a spring of water welling up to eternal life" (4:13–14).

The scribes and Pharisees of the day had developed a lifestyle of blame and condemnation. No respectable Jew would ever be caught associating with the lost and rejected of society. Sinners were to be excommunicated for their sin, not acknowledged.

But Jesus didn't see it that way. Jesus loved people in spite of their sin, and he cared deeply for them, regardless of the baggage they brought to the table. He saw people not as they were but as they were meant to be. And because of it, his love was unconditional, resolute, and life-altering.

Too often you and I find ourselves in the condemning business. Like the Pharisees, we spend much of our time hanging out with people just like us. People who are respectable and proper and who go to the right church. People who speak our language and relate to our lifestyle. People who are pleasant and likable and enjoyable to be around.

And when someone like Ralph comes into our world—someone smelly and messy and unlikable—we don't quite know what to do with them. So we look the other way. We steer clear of them. We shun them, not necessarily with our words but with our actions.

And like the woman at the well, they quickly learn their place in proper society. They learn to fetch their water at noon, in the heat of the day, when all the righteous people are finished filling their buckets. They avoid us the same way we've avoided them.

Time and again in Scripture we see the scribes and Pharisees condemning Jesus for associating with sinners. "Why does your teacher eat with tax collectors and sinners?" they asked his apostles (Matt. 9:11).

And the answer Jesus gave them should be carved atop the doorway of every Christian church we build: "It is not the healthy who need a doctor, but the sick. . . . For I have not come to call the righteous, but sinners" (vv. 12–13).

The Right to Be Heard

During my time at Reading University, I quickly learned how futile it is to try to share the Good News with people before first gaining their trust. I came to the United Kingdom as an outsider, an American who was dubbed by some as a "Bible thumper." Most students I met just laughed at me when I tried to talk about Jesus. My first few months, I experienced a lot of frustration and defeat. People seemed to like me, but they didn't take me very seriously. "You really believe all that nonsense?" they would ask as they laughed and waved me off.

I learned that if I ever hoped to reach anyone for Jesus, I would have to first step into their world. To become their friend. To hang out with them and get to know them on a personal level. I learned that the best way to gain someone's ear is to first gain their trust. I had to earn the right to be heard. So I threw myself into the lives of the students I encountered.

I had grown up playing sports, so I naturally gravitated toward the campus athletes. Since I was an American, they didn't expect me to know much about soccer or squash, but I quickly proved them wrong. I wasn't the best player on the field, but I stuck it out and held my own. Even I was surprised at how well I was able to keep up with the other players.

And when it came to table tennis, I earned the right to play number one on the college team. I honestly can't remember anyone in England beating me the entire time I was there.

I gained the students' respect, and along with it they gave me their trust. Also, because I had done my homework and had found strong evidence to back up my beliefs, students were open to listening and began coming to Jesus on a regular basis. More often than not, they would be the ones to instigate the conversation. They knew I was a Christian, and most of them had never hung out with believers, so they were instinctively curious about my faith.

I was the one they came to with their questions because I was the only follower of Jesus they trusted.

Loving the Unlovable

This may not be the most profound principle of evangelism, but it is likely the most critical. If we ever hope to reach people with the Good News of Jesus, we have to first learn to accept them as they are, not as we wish they would be.

The people who most need Jesus are often the most unkempt and unlikable people we know. They are the women who draw water at the well at noon in order to avoid the stares and whispers of the Pharisees. They are the Ralphs of the world who curse and smoke and refuse to shave in order to keep "proper" people at a safe distance.

They are the men in your office who don't know Jesus, but they know you're a believer, so they steer clear of you when putting together a foursome for golf. They are the women in your neighborhood who don't make eye contact when walking down the street, because they see you leave for church every Sunday and they've been judged one too many times already. They are the unmarried couple at the end of your block that you would never consider inviting to a barbecue, because they'd probably just feel uncomfortable anyway.

These are the people in your world who most need Jesus. But first they need a friend like you. Someone who isn't afraid to associate with those who might feel uncomfortable in a religious setting. Someone who remembers what it was like to be lost and alone and unwanted. Someone who will love and accept them as they are, no matter what baggage they bring to the table.

Friendship Evangelism

While living in Reading, I got a call from one of the longtime campus ministers at a nearby university. He asked if he could spend a few days with me on campus, just to see what I was doing. I wasn't sure why, because he didn't seem too happy with me, but I agreed to let him tag along.

The first day we were together, I asked him about his request. He said to me, "Well, I've been here a long time, and I know I'm smarter than you. I'm also smarter than most of the students here on campus. When I witness to them, I win every argument we get into. I'm convinced that I can out-argue any student on campus. But no one ever seems to want to begin a relationship with Jesus, and I don't understand why. From what I hear, quite a few of the students you talk to come to Jesus, so I want to find out what you're doing and how you're doing it."

I just smiled and took him to a small table in the student center, and the two of us spent the day discussing the principle of friendship evangelism.

I can defend my faith against even the most brutal inquisition, but that's not what people care about. I can probably stand a good chance of debunking a die-hard atheist's views in a debate, but what good does that do if I don't know how to make him feel loved and accepted by God?

In all my years as a believer, I've never known anyone who came to Jesus because they lost an argument. But I've known countless people who surrendered their lives to Christ because someone cared enough to love them into the kingdom.

Jesus loved people in spite of their sin. And he saw them not as they were but as they were created to be.

Shouldn't you and I do the same?

8

He Would Show Them
That He Cared

By this everyone will know that you are my disciples, if you love one another.

—John 13:35

Doug came to Stanford on a football scholarship. He was a highly touted player with a promising career, and the coaches were thrilled to have him. I met him early in his freshman season, but when he found out I was a believer, he quickly started avoiding me at every opportunity.

That's something I see a fair amount of in my work at Stanford. Kids often come to college to get away from the watchful eyes of their parents, and the last thing they want is a stereotyped goody-goody looking over their shoulder. I understood Doug's reticence, but I continued to reach out to him whenever I could.

For four years Doug avoided talking to me. Often I'd pass him on the field and try to strike up a conversation, but he'd just pretend he didn't hear and slip into the locker room. When I'd see him in the student union, he'd go out of his way to keep from making eye contact.

That always made me sad, because I knew that his football career had been plagued with injuries on the field, and I wanted the chance to help him through those months of frustration. But he never let me get close, no matter how many times I approached him.

Then one day, during his senior year, I was walking down the sidewalk in front of the student union and heard my name. I turned around and there stood Doug, looking me right in the eyes. It was the first time in four years he'd even spoken to me.

"Hello, Doug," I said. "What can I do for you?"

He glanced at the ground for a second, gathering his thoughts, then said, "I just heard that my mother has cancer, and they don't expect her to live very long. I want to help my dad, but I don't know what to do. Can we please talk?"

"Of course we can," I told him, and we set a meeting for the next day.

During our visit, I learned that Doug had grown up going to church from time to time, but his parents were not very faithful, and neither was Doug. He had little use for spiritual matters. But he told me he had often thought about God and wondered what he really believed, especially since his football career didn't turn out the way he had expected. His numerous injuries had ruined any hope he had of playing professional football, and he had no idea what his future would hold.

I spent much of our first couple of times together just listening to Doug talk about his struggles and his fear of losing his mother at such a young age. I knew that he'd had a rough four years, but I had no idea how much anxiety and confusion he'd been dealing with.

During our third meeting together, Doug accepted Jesus as his Lord and Savior. It was exciting to see him finally surrendering his life to God after building so many walls to keep his heart guarded.

Passing It On

Doug and I had been studying through a small booklet titled *Would You Like to Know God Personally?*, and after he accepted Jesus, I gave him a handful of copies to keep. I encouraged him to read through them with his friends when opportunities arose.

He and I continued to meet each week, and it was thrilling to see how rapidly he began to grow in his faith. Often when we'd get together, he'd spend time praying for his friends who didn't know Jesus, and especially for his mother. He told me he knew his mother believed in God, but he didn't think she had a real relationship with Jesus, and he was deeply worried about her eternal fate.

When the fall quarter ended, Doug went home to be with his family and to help get his mother's affairs in order. He was there for only a few weeks when I got a frantic call from him late one evening.

"My mother is going downhill fast," he told me, "and the doctors don't think she will last more than a few days. I really want her to have a relationship with Jesus before she dies, but I don't think she'll listen to me. Can you please come out here and tell her about Jesus the way you told me?"

I would have given anything to fly out to the Midwest to meet him, but my schedule simply wouldn't allow it. So I said to him, "Doug, you know what to say. You have that booklet I gave you. Just read through that with her and explain the Good News the best you can. I know she'll listen to you."

Doug was in a state of panic. "But I've never done that on my own, and I don't want to practice on my mom. This is too important! What if I say the wrong thing?"

I calmed him down as best I could and assured him that he'd do fine. "Trust me, Doug. You're a Stanford graduate. You can read. Your mother will listen to you. Just read through the booklet with her and explain to her who Jesus is and what he means to you. I know you can do this."

We prayed together before hanging up the phone. The next day he called me and excitedly told me what had happened. He had taken my advice and gone to the hospital to sit with his mom that evening, and while there he began reading through the small booklet with her. He told me his mom had never understood how to have a relationship with Jesus.

"I asked if she wanted to accept Jesus into her heart, and she said yes," Doug told me. "So we prayed together as she gave her life to Christ. She died just a few hours later, but I'm so excited to know that she will be in heaven waiting for me!"

Doug's voice lifted with joy as he relayed the entire story to me exactly as it had happened. It was an exciting conversation for both of us. Not only was he able to lead his mother to Jesus, but he was able to rest in the assurance of his mother's secure eternity in heaven with Jesus.

The Commitment to Be Available

A very fun yet important aspect of my ministry is to show every football player that I am available and that I care about them. So every afternoon during preseason and in season, I hang out on the sidelines whenever the Stanford team is practicing. I am a regular fixture at the practice field. Everyone on the team knows me by name because I'm always there, cheering my guys on.

I don't do this just because I love sports, though I'm sure a lot of people might think that's the case. I want the guys I'm mentoring to know how much I care about their daily lives and how invested I am in our mentoring relationship. So when I meet with individual players later, I know exactly what's going on with them—the great play they made, the teammate who was injured, the bad day on the field—and I can provide counsel, perspective, and prayer.

I consider my time observing each practice as one of the most critical parts of my ministry. It's an investment of time that I'm willing to make because I've seen the results firsthand. Not only does it show the guys I mentor how much I care about their lives, but other players see me on the sidelines and they know I'm available if they ever need me. Many of these players may not know Jesus yet, but they know that if they're ever curious about spiritual matters, I'm someone they can come to.

Still today I'm continually surprised by how often that happens.

Wayne's Story

Wayne was another player with no interest in spiritual matters. In fact, his interests were anything but spiritual. He was a huge young man, a linebacker who came to Stanford on a football scholarship. And he was as mean and unruly as any player on the team. He was known for saying that his goal was to sleep with more women than any guy who had ever been to Stanford. And from what I'd heard, he was well on his way to achieving that goal.

Wayne also drank so much that it was impossible to tell whether he was drunk or sober at any given time. He was loud and flamboyant and rowdy.

For the first year and a half, Wayne avoided me on campus. He would often say hi, but he was never willing to engage in conversation.

Then one day, I was sitting at my regular table in the café, meeting for the first time with one of the star baseball players on campus. He wasn't yet a believer, but he had asked if he could meet with me. He was a shy and polite young man, and I was looking forward to getting to know him better. We had just started talking when I looked up and there stood Wayne, towering over us.

He interrupted our conversation without apology and said to me, "They told me I'm supposed to start meeting with you, so how do we do that?"

His question startled me. "Who told you that?" I asked.

"Just some of my teammates," he answered. "They told me I should start meeting with you, so I need to know how we're supposed to do that."

I happened to have an available hour in my schedule at the time, so we set a date for the next afternoon.

During our first meeting, Wayne was as nervous as any kid I'd ever seen. I could tell he was sober, but he couldn't stop fidgeting. His legs kept bouncing and moving. I engaged in small talk for a few minutes, hoping it might calm him down.

Finally he said to me, "So, what are we supposed to do? What am I supposed to say?"

I smiled and said, "Well, why don't you begin by telling me why you wanted to start meeting with me."

"I don't really know," he said. "The other guys just kept telling me that I need to meet with you, and I was curious about what you do, so that's why I'm here. I don't know what to say or what we're supposed to do, but they said I needed to talk to you, so here I am."

I was surprised that he took his friends' advice but glad that he did. So I started the conversation the way I always begin meetings with new students. "Let's just take some time to get to know each other," I told him. "Why don't you tell me a little about yourself and what brought you to Stanford, then I'll tell you about my journey."

The more Wayne talked about his life, the calmer he became. Soon he was completely relaxed and comfortable with me. We had a great time visiting, and before long our hour was almost up.

Before ending our meeting, I said to him, "Wayne, I don't know where you are in your spiritual journey, but I want to be honest with you up front. If you'd like to keep meeting with me, I'm happy to do that. But my goal is to teach you about how to become a follower of Jesus. You're a bright guy, and I know you're going to want to follow him once you discover who he is and what he's done for you. I don't know when you're going to decide that, but when you do, I want you to have all the evidence you need to make an informed decision. I'd love to begin meeting with you each week to talk about Jesus, but only if you're willing."

He agreed to continue meeting with me, so we set a time and day for the following week. We began reading through the booklet *Would You Like to Know God Personally?*, and at one point Wayne told me he had never heard the gospel message, even though he had grown up around a lot of Christian friends and schoolmates. "No one has ever told me the story of Jesus," he said.

The next week he came with even more questions about Jesus, and I answered them the best I could. It was exciting to see how engaged and interested he was in learning more. Toward the end of our meeting I said to him, "Wayne, I know this won't make much sense to you, but a lot of the questions you have can only be understood through the power of the Holy Spirit. God promises to send the Holy Spirit to help us once we surrender our lives to Jesus. I want to encourage you to think about becoming a follower of Jesus and inviting him into your life. Once you do that, a lot of things will become clearer to you. I don't want to push you before you're ready. It's just something I want you to think about this week."

Wayne took my advice, and the next time we met, he told me he was ready to accept Jesus as his Lord and Savior. The two of us bowed our heads and prayed as he asked Jesus into his heart.

Wayne and I continued to meet throughout the rest of his time at Stanford, and each week I watched his faith grow deeper and stronger. Soon he had turned into a powerful force for God on the Stanford football team. He began witnessing to his friends and teammates, and by the time he graduated, he had led numerous other players to Christ.

Today Wayne plays professional football and is one of the most outspoken Christians on his team. He and I still stay in touch on a regular basis. He's one of the most encouraging friends I have, and he's widely respected by the other players.

When I talk to him today, I still find it hard to believe that he is the same gruff and unkempt young man who interrupted my meeting those many years ago. Today he is nothing like that. He is truly a new creation in Christ. God has done a miraculous work in his heart and life!

It's All about Relationships

If there was one overarching message about bringing others to Jesus that I could relay to the body of Christ, it would be this: *Sharing Jesus is all about relationships.*

It isn't about getting people saved or filling another pew in the sanctuary. It isn't about getting someone's name on a "decision card" or getting them to recite a prayer. It's about building the kingdom of God one relationship at a time. It's about growing disciples, teaching them how to live for Jesus, and then sending them out to disciple others.

It's about making yourself available to those who don't know Jesus, and then being there when they're ready to talk.

The Holy Spirit is constantly working to draw people into a relationship with God. He is always convicting and prodding and wooing them to seek out the truth about Jesus. And when people are ready, the Holy Spirit steers them toward someone who can help them take the next step in their spiritual journey.

That's why it is so important to be there when your friends' hearts begin to soften. To be available with open arms and an inviting smile. To love them into the kingdom by showing how much you care.

Just Show That You Care

Years ago, while working in the United Kingdom, I attended a small church near the Reading campus. The pastor there didn't seem to like me too much. I wasn't sure why until one Sunday morning when he decided to confront me. He told me he thought I had no business coming from America to try to "proselytize" British students, and he was sure I was doing more harm than good. He was afraid I would disrupt his church's ministry to students and might even turn them away from the church. I assured him that I would do my best not to get in the way of any outreach programs the church had going.

After that, I tried to stay out of his way, but I continued attending his church. And each time I helped lead a student to Jesus, I'd begin bringing them to church on Sunday morning. Within a few months, I had so many students coming with me that we filled up the first three rows of the sanctuary.

One day the pastor came to me again and said, "I guess I was wrong about you. I have to say, whatever you're doing, it must be working. I'm not sure what I think of these four spiritual laws you talk about, but maybe I need to start using that same approach."

I didn't have the heart to tell him at the time, but I don't think it was the method that made the difference.

Sharing Jesus is all about relationships. It's about loving people into the kingdom one person at a time. As the old cliché goes, "People don't care how much you know until they know how much you care!"

9

He Would Teach Them How to Pray

Lord, teach us to pray.

—Luke 11:1

Unless I had the spirit of prayer, I could do nothing.

—Charles Finney

During my early years at Stanford, I had a number of young athletes meeting with me each week. I was only a few years older than some of the guys I was mentoring, and there was a lot of trial and error in my approach. I was still working to find the best way to disciple young believers in their faith.

My daily schedule was completely booked, so I decided to start a football team Bible study one evening a week. I really enjoyed the team study because it gave everyone a chance to get to know each other in a different setting and interact in a meaningful way.

It wasn't as intimate as a mentoring session, but it was a great way to build camaraderie among the athletes.

During one of our group studies, one young man asked me, "How are we supposed to pray?"

"What do you mean?" I asked him.

"Well, I know we're supposed to pray, but what are we supposed to pray for? And how do we go about it?"

His question caught me a bit off guard. I had grown up watching my godly parents pray every day, so when I gave my heart to Jesus, praying came naturally to me. I spent a lot of my time praying for the guys I mentored, as well as every other aspect of my life, so I just assumed everyone knew how to do it.

"Those are good questions," I said. "Why don't we take a few weeks and do a study on prayer?" And that's what we did. We started digging into the Scriptures each week to see what the Bible had to say about prayer. I actually had never realized how much I didn't know about prayer until we began to study it in depth.

Then one day, several weeks into our study, I decided it was time to try out what we had learned. I brought some paper and pencils with me to the study and passed them out among the guys.

"I have an assignment for you," I said. "I want each of you to write down the names of three people on the team who you think would never come to Jesus. We will call them 'the Impossibles.' Tear the paper in half and write down the names on both pieces, then pass one to me and keep the other one for your wallet."

I was surprised by how quickly the guys began writing down names. Most of them didn't even have to think about it; they just scribbled three names on their papers and passed one copy to me.

When all the papers were in, I glanced through them and was amazed to see that almost every guy had written the same three names. I read the names aloud and looked up to see everyone in the room smiling and nodding. They agreed unanimously that these three guys were the most rowdy and lost players on the team.

"Here's what we're going to do," I said. "Let's all commit to begin praying specifically for these three guys over the next few years. Let's pray that God would soften their hearts and bring them to salvation. I really believe God is going to do a miracle and answer our prayers. Let's begin believing him for this miracle and then see what happens."

Even as the words left my lips, I could feel the sweat forming on my brow. It was a huge leap of faith on my part, but I really wanted to show these men the power of prayer. *Dear Lord*, I prayed silently, *please hear our prayers and bring these three men to faith. I don't want these guys to feel let down.*

I secretly hoped I hadn't overstepped my bounds.

Ben's Story

Stanford had a great football season that year, and we eventually found ourselves in the coliseum playing the USC Trojans in one of the last games of the season. It was an evening game, so our chapel service was scheduled for earlier that afternoon for those who wanted to attend. The players were staying in one of the nicer hotels in Los Angeles, so we decided to meet in one of the players' rooms.

About twenty-five of us showed up for the chapel service that afternoon, and we crammed into the room shoulder to shoulder. We were packed in like sardines, but just before we started, the door opened and one last guy squeezed through the door. My mouth nearly dropped to the floor when I saw who it was. It was Ben, the first of the three guys we'd been praying for on the list.

Without saying a word, he quietly slipped through the crowd and found an empty spot on one of the beds on the far side of the room. Then he hurriedly sat down and put his head in his hands, trying hard not to draw attention to himself. You could hear a pin drop as every guy in the room held his breath, waiting for me to begin.

Ben sat still through the entire service. He never once moved or looked up.

Thirty minutes later we ended the service with a prayer, and as soon as I said, "Amen," he was off the bed and out of the room like he'd been shot out of a cannon.

We all sat in a state of shock. Guys started glancing around the room at each other, many whispering to each other under their breath. And I knew we were all thinking the same thing.

Did that just happen?

Stanford handily beat USC that night, and with about two minutes left on the clock, I was making my way up the sidelines congratulating the guys one by one for their win. I was slapping guys on the back, saying, "Great game! Way to play out there," trying not to get crushed by all the huge bodies, when suddenly I heard footsteps coming up behind me. I turned to see Ben standing right in front of me. He was a huge human being, and I had to look nearly straight up to see his face.

He reached his massive hands out toward me, and I didn't know whether to duck or run. He grabbed me by the shoulders and literally lifted me off my feet in order to look me in the eyes. Then he said, "Jim, my life is really a mess right now. Could we get together and talk sometime?"

I struggled to take a breath and said to him, "Of course we can, Ben. How about tomorrow afternoon?" I'm not sure if I was more shocked by his request or more relieved that he didn't hit me.

During our meeting the next day, Ben completely opened up to me. He fought back tears the entire time as he told me how much he had been struggling over the past few months. God had obviously been pursuing his heart and working to bring him to conviction.

He told me he had never known the story of Jesus as I shared the gospel message with him. He was mesmerized by the story of the cross.

We decided to meet again the next day to continue our discussion, then again the day after that. It was during our third meeting that Ben asked if he could pray and accept Jesus as his Lord and Savior.

I couldn't wait to share this exciting news with the guys in my Bible study.

Sammy's Story

The news of Ben's newfound faith quickly spread around the Stanford team. I'm not sure a lot of players believed it, given Ben's well-earned reputation, but those who knew him immediately began to see the difference in his life. Each week he and I would meet together to pray and study, and even I was amazed at his transformation. He was truly serious about his new walk with the Lord.

One day Ben was in the locker room before practice when another player cornered him. It was Sammy, his best friend on the team. Sammy also happened to be the second person on the list of guys we'd been praying for.

Sammy poked Ben in the chest with his finger and said, "Hey, I heard you became a Christian. Is that true?"

"Yes, it's true," Ben answered.

Sammy stiffened his neck and said sarcastically, "Well, isn't that sweet? What are you going to do now, kiss me?"

Ben obliged him. Almost by reflex, he "kissed" him smack in the middle of his left cheek with a quick and powerful right hook. It probably wasn't the most loving response, but it was the last time Sammy teased him about his faith.

Sammy was well known by most students on campus. He called himself "The Producer" and could often be seen wearing an old French beret around campus. He also owned a tall folding chair, like the ones used by movie directors, and he took it with him almost everywhere he went.

Sammy did this because he was in the business of producing inappropriate films and selling them under the table to other students on campus.

Sammy had the reputation of being one of the sleaziest students on campus. And he only seemed to get worse as time went by. But our Bible study group continued to pray for him, believing that God would somehow move in his heart.

After graduation, Sammy played in the NFL for a few years, but most of us completely lost track of him. We still prayed for him regularly, both in private and during our studies, but we had no idea how—or if—our prayers were being answered.

Some years later, I was invited to attend a special Rose Bowl event where players from the early seventies were being given special recognition. The event became something of a mini reunion for those of us who had been on the sidelines during those years. I was able to connect with a lot of the guys I had mentored during that time.

During the reception, a handful of us were standing to one side, laughing and reminiscing about the good old days. Suddenly I looked up and there was Sammy. He was smiling from ear to ear, striding across the room at a quick pace. His massive frame almost shook the room as he lunged toward me.

He gave me a huge bear hug, then said, "Jim Stump! I'm so glad to see you!"

"Good to see you too, Sammy," I said, gasping for air.

He let go and stood in the middle of the group, still smiling. "Tell me," he said, "are you still at Stanford talking to athletes about Jesus?"

"Yes, I am," I answered.

"That's so great to hear," he said. "Promise me you'll never stop doing that. They really need you there."

I was completely floored by his comments. And so were most of the guys standing with me. Without skipping a beat, Sammy began sharing his testimony. He told us that after playing several years in the NFL, he moved to Florida with his family, and while there he made money on the side growing and selling marijuana. Little had changed since his days on campus. Until one day his son died in a freak accident and he went into a severe depression.

"It really affected me deeply," he said. "I was so depressed, I seriously considered suicide."

Then one day a hippie walked through the neighborhood, saw him outside, and struck up a conversation with him. The young man told him about Jesus and shared the Good News with him.

"He led me to the Lord that day, and I've never looked back," Sammy said.

He also told us that he had just started his first year of seminary and was studying to become a minister.

Several of the guys standing with us had been in the Bible study group with me back when Sammy was in college, and their eyes lit up with excitement as he told us his story. All these years later we learned that our prayers had been answered.

Jason's Story

The third player on our prayer list was a student named Jason. He was a quiet young man who rarely talked, except when he was cursing or telling someone off. He was a mean and brutal player on the field, with a bad temper and biceps the size of tree trunks.

Jason never said a word to me the entire time he was at Stanford. Whenever he saw me on the sidelines, he'd turn and walk the other way. It was obvious he wasn't interested in hearing anything I had to say. I often tried to strike up conversations with him, but to no avail.

Still, each time our group met, we'd pray for Jason. And we also kept him in our personal prayers. We all believed God for a miracle in his life.

Jason, too, graduated and went to play in the NFL, and soon I lost track of him. Several years went by and I hadn't heard much about him. Until one day, nearly twenty years later, I was attending practice at Stanford and saw him standing on the far side of the field. He looked up and our eyes met, and this time he didn't look away, as he had so many times before.

Not wanting to be rude, I decided to walk across the field to say hi. As I got closer I could see him smiling at me. And to my surprise, he was wearing a Promise Keepers T-shirt.

"Jim, I can't believe you're still here," he said as I approached him. It was the first time he'd ever spoken to me. Then he said something that really took me by surprise: "Praise the Lord!"

We exchanged hugs and he excitedly began to tell me his story. After a number of successful years in the NFL, he got caught in the middle of a huge pileup during a play-off game and accidentally got kicked in the head. He blacked out and woke up in a hospital bed with a brace around his neck and shoulders. He couldn't move his head in either direction and had almost no memory of what had happened.

The doctors told him he'd suffered a severe brain aneurysm. In order to give himself a chance of staying alive, he needed to stay in his brace, flat on his back, until the swelling went down. They had no idea how long that would take, only that the recovery would likely be long and painful.

"The only way I could look was up," he said, "so I lay there in that hospital room, staring at the ceiling, day after day."

It was during this time that all the memories of his days at Stanford came flooding to the surface. And what he remembered most were the conversations about Jesus he would hear in the locker room each day after practice. The guys I mentored would often use their time in the locker room to pray together and encourage each other in their faith, and Jason would silently be listening as he showered and dressed each day.

"All those conversations came to mind as I lay in that hospital bed," he said. "I had always admired those guys and often wished I knew their secret. So one day I decided to pray and see if God was for real. I prayed, 'Lord, I don't know if you're there, and I've done a lot of bad things in my life, but if you'll still have me, I want to follow you.'"

The entire time he was in the hospital, he continued to pray that God would accept him, and when he got out, the first thing he did was to seek out a church to attend. It was there that he began to fall in love with Jesus and develop a deep and meaningful faith.

"Today I'm the assistant pastor of a church in Texas," he told me, "and I'm in my second year of seminary. I hope to be a senior pastor someday."

It was so exciting to hear Jason's testimony. And the entire time he talked, all I could think about were those many hours we had spent praying on his behalf. He had no idea that he was one of three players we had committed to pray for during those years, and I couldn't wait to share that fact with him.

I also couldn't wait to get home and write to the other men from our original Bible study group to tell them what God had accomplished through our prayers!

The Faith of a Mustard Seed

One day Jesus was teaching his disciples, and they presented him with a request: "Increase our faith!" (Luke 17:5).

The disciples were beginning to understand the plans Jesus had for their future, and they felt inadequate for the task. They instinctively knew that they wouldn't be able to accomplish the things God wanted them to do in their own power, and they were likely afraid of what might happen if their faith proved too weak. It's a fear that almost every believer has experienced at one time or another. We all long to do great things for God, but we know our faith is often frail and fickle.

Jesus responded to their request by saying, "If you have faith as small as a mustard seed, you can say to this mulberry tree, 'Be uprooted and planted in the sea,' and it will obey you" (v. 6).

In effect he was telling them, "Even things that seem impossible become possible if you just have enough faith that God can accomplish them."

Sometime later the disciples came to Jesus again with a similar concern. They were unable to heal a demon-possessed young boy, so Jesus came to their aid and cast the demon out. The disciples asked him, "Why couldn't we drive it out?" (Matt. 17:19).

Jesus told them, "Because you have so little faith" (v. 20).

Then he reiterated what he had told them earlier about the importance of believing in God's power: "Truly I tell you, if you have faith as small as a mustard seed, you can say to this mountain, 'Move from here to there,' and it will move. Nothing will be impossible for you" (v. 20).

Of all the lessons Jesus wanted his disciples to learn, this one was at the top of the list. He wanted them to understand that God is in the business of moving mountains. That nothing is impossible for God. And when we walk in his will, we become active participants with him in that power. We get to see the impossible become possible.

Through faith, we get to see God do things that none of us could comprehend or accomplish on our own. And prayer is the way we express our faith. When we pray big prayers, we're saying to God, "I know I could never move this mountain on my own, but you can. I truly believe that you want this mountain moved, so I'm trusting you for a miracle!"

Through prayer, not only do we express our faith in God's power to accomplish great things, but we also become active partners with him in the process. We come alongside God as he teaches us the ins and outs of the mountain-moving business.

And don't all of us have at least one mountain in our life that needs moving?

We are all in contact with at least one person we truly can't imagine ever coming to Jesus. One person who appears so distant, so angry, so lost, so ambivalent to God's grace that we're certain they will never come to faith. We're so sure of it that not only have we given up reaching out to them, but they've long since been crossed off our prayer list.

Maybe it's your best friend from high school, or the angry neighbor down the street, or the guy who works a few cubicles away from you at the office. Maybe it's your boss, or the kid who does your lawn. Maybe it's someone closer to your heart, like a wayward daughter or an unbelieving nephew.

Whoever that person is in your life, let me encourage you to begin believing God for a miracle. Write their name in the front of your Bible and then commit to praying daily that God would begin to soften their hearts. Pray that he would give you the faith to keep praying, even when it feels like you're wasting your breath. Then pray that he would give you the opportunity to reach out to them when the time is right.

There is no mountain that God can't move. And there is no human being on the planet that he doesn't long to bring into relationship with him. Begin today believing God for a miracle, and then watch what he can accomplish through your mustard seed of faith.

10

He Would Always Tell the Truth

I am the way and the truth and the life. No one comes to the Father except through me.

—John 14:6

For I am not ashamed of the gospel, because it is the power of God that brings salvation to everyone who believes.

—Romans 1:16

During my second year in England, I was put into contact with the head of Special Services for the Air Force at Ruislip Air Force Base in the United Kingdom. His name was Jim Murray, and he had once played linebacker for the Los Angeles Rams.

I was serving as the European director of Athletes in Action at the time, and a mutual friend thought we would hit it off, so he said I should get to know him. I love making new friends, so I took him up on his offer and gave Jim a call.

Jim was a jovial guy who had a hearty laugh and a bucketful of memorable stories, and we had a great time sharing football tales on the phone. At one point he asked what I was doing in England, and I told him I was working with Athletes in Action, but before I could explain what I actually did, he interrupted me in mid-sentence and asked, "What are you doing this weekend?"

I told him my schedule was clear, so he said, "We are hosting the European Services Wrestling Championships next week, and we're kicking it off this Friday with a banquet. Our keynote speaker just canceled. How would you like to fill in for us?"

I swallowed hard and said, "Yes, I think I can do that."

I had no idea what I was going to say or what kind of crowd it was going to be, but I've learned that when the Lord opens a door, it's our job to take a deep breath and walk through it, even if we don't know what's on the other side.

Not Your Sunday Morning Crowd

I drove two and a half hours through the plush and winding English countryside to get to the base. I had just purchased a used, robin's-egg-blue Morris Minor convertible, and the heater decided to stop working the first ten minutes of the drive, so I arrived nearly frozen. My face was numb, and I had to pry my fingers off the steering wheel to get out of the car.

I made my way through several huge buildings, stopping a couple of times to ask directions, and eventually found my way to the banquet hall. There were about a hundred wrestlers milling around, waiting for the event to start. I learned that most of them hadn't eaten all day, since they had to weigh in for the competition earlier that afternoon, so they were starting to get impatient. Several were already in their seats, staring at the kitchen doors, waiting for the food to be served.

I made my way to the head table and immediately recognized Jim's voice as he stood joking with a general. I introduced myself, and he in turn introduced me to the general as well as to a lieutenant colonel standing next to him, both of whom were scheduled to speak that evening. I could sense the two of them sizing me up, wondering who I was and why I was chosen to speak. It was a military event, and I was clearly not a military guy. I just smiled and tried to look like I belonged there.

The general kicked off the event by welcoming everyone to the banquet, and then he commenced to tell several off-color stories to loosen up the troops. The lieutenant colonel followed his speech with a few risqué stories of his own, several laced with profanity and innuendos. The crowd loved it. With every racy punch line the room would explode with laughter. And the longer he talked, the worse it got. Every story seemed to be raunchier than the one before. This was obviously not your Sunday morning crowd.

The lieutenant colonel finished, and Jim stood to introduce me. I'm not even sure what he said, because I was busy praying fervently for wisdom and favor. I had some thoughts and stories prepared, but I had put them together before realizing what a rough audience this was going to be. These guys clearly hadn't come here tonight expecting to hear about Jesus.

As I stood at the podium, looking out over the crowd of muscle-bound wrestlers, I thought, *You may never have this opportunity again. Just be bold. The worst they can do is throw you out the back door.*

I was just glad most of them had already eaten by that point of the evening.

I began by telling them a little about Athletes in Action. The AIA wrestling team had just defeated the defending Olympic champion Japanese team in a match, so I knew that would impress them. I told them about our mission and purpose as a ministry and then began sharing my own personal testimony. I talked about my spiritual journey and how I became a follower of Jesus. Then I shared the Good News as clearly as I knew how.

The longer I spoke, the more I felt the boldness of the Holy Spirit welling up within me. I decided to hold nothing back. I told them how Jesus died on the cross for our sins in order to bring us into relationship with him, and I shared what it means to become a follower of Jesus. Then I closed by saying, "In a minute I'm going to pray, and I invite anyone who wants to follow Jesus to pray along with me. If you'd like to invite Jesus into your heart and make him your Lord and Savior, then pray this prayer silently with me, asking him to come into your life."

There was a quiet solemnness in the room as I prayed aloud, leading the entire crowd in a prayer of salvation. When I finished, I thanked them for listening, then backed into my seat beside the general. I wondered what he was thinking. I half expected him to have me handcuffed and arrested for insubordination, but instead he sat silently.

After a few minutes I summoned the courage to look in his direction, and I noticed several small tears rolling down his cheek. He turned to me and said, "For the past fifty-two years I've needed to hear what you had to say. I want you to know that I prayed along with you tonight and invited Jesus to come into my life. I want to follow him."

He and I had a great conversation that evening, and he asked me more about what it means to be a follower of Jesus. Then we set a date for me to return to the base for a game of squash and an afternoon of spiritual conversation. We became good friends over the next few months.

Jim and Nancy Murray

Jim closed the evening with a few announcements and then immediately came over to talk to me. "I'm not sure anyone was expecting that," he said, chuckling. I was glad to see he wasn't offended.

He told me that the infamous London fog had rolled in, so he invited me to stay at his house until morning. "It's not safe to drive home at night on these winding roads," he said. "Besides, I'd like my wife and family to meet you."

I'd already been dreading the cold drive, so I gladly took him up on his offer.

His wife, Nancy, and their five children were waiting up for us when we got to his home. Jim introduced his kids and then quickly scooted them off to bed. Nancy invited Jim and me into the den, where she had a pot of hot coffee waiting.

"So, Jim, what do you do, and what brings you to these parts?" Nancy asked.

Even as the words left her mouth, I could sense her husband tensing up. He chuckled nervously and fidgeted in his seat. I told Nancy about my work with Athletes in Action, and that our goal was to spread the Good News and bring people into a personal relationship with Jesus.

Her back stiffened as I spoke. "Well, we go to church every Sunday," she said.

"That's great to hear!" I responded. "So you're a follower of Jesus?"

That's when things got awkward. She immediately began telling me about the liturgy and traditions of her church, and how faithful she and her family had been in attending. But the longer she talked, the more I realized how little she truly understood about her faith.

It's a dynamic I saw a lot during my time in England. A number of people I ran across attended church regularly, but that was the extent of their loyalty. They attended more out of obligation than spiritual conviction. Often when I would speak of having a real and personal relationship with Jesus, most had no idea what I was talking about.

It soon became clear that Jim and Nancy were in that category. Much of what I explained about Jesus seemed completely foreign to them. It was an interesting conversation, and I did my best to be polite but honest. At one point I excused myself and retrieved my Bible from the car, then I began sharing passages from the words of Jesus that explained the purpose of the cross and the way to salvation. It was obvious that neither of them had ever heard the good news of the gospel message.

The longer we spoke, the more I could sense Nancy closing off to me. I could almost see the walls erecting between us. So I said to her, "Do you want to hear something unbelievable? I grew up going to church every week. In fact, my parents were missionaries, and we had church services in the living room of our home. Every Sunday I heard my dad talk about Jesus, but I never quite got it. I didn't understand what it meant to have a personal relationship with Jesus until I was twenty-two years old."

Then I shared my testimony. I told them about my childhood, my years at Wheaton College, and the day Bud Hinkson invited me to join his University Ambassador Team in California. Then I recapped the day I heard the story of Jesus explained in a way that I never had before. "It was the first time in my life that I truly understood the sacrifice Jesus made on the cross," I said. "So I asked Jesus into my heart, and my life has never again been the same. I still find it hard to believe that I could have spent my entire life going to church and yet never truly understood how to meet the person of Jesus."

We talked until two in the morning, and though I had answered many questions, I still wasn't entirely sure how my words were being received. As I lay in bed that night, I realized that I might have offended these two wonderful people who took me into their home, and I felt bad about that. But I knew I had done the right thing. I had committed to Jesus that I would always be truthful when sharing the Good News, even if people were offended by the message.

I thought of the passage where Peter wrote, "Always be prepared to give an answer to everyone who asks you to give the reason for the hope that you have. But do this with gentleness and respect" (1 Pet. 3:15). I hoped I had reflected that attitude, but I didn't know for sure.

Dear Lord, I prayed, *please give Jim and Nancy an understanding of your grace and goodness. Help them know that I wasn't trying to be offensive. But please open their eyes to the true depth of your love.*

The Offense of the Gospel

By its very nature, the gospel is an offensive message. Jesus said it would be, and the disciples discovered firsthand how right he was. Every one of them suffered persecution for their faith, and most were killed because of it. The world was offended by Jesus because he brought a message that many were not willing to hear. Those living in sin don't want to be reminded of the consequences of their sin. And those who try to get to heaven on their own merit don't want to hear that it can't be done. The message was true then, and it's still true today.

One of the toughest tightropes we walk as believers is learning how to proclaim the offensive truth of the Good News without irreparably offending those who need to hear it. Sometimes it simply can't be done.

The gospel of Jesus is riddled with hard truths that can easily turn people away.

The gospel tells us that our works will never be enough to save us. That none of us are righteous. That no matter how hard we try, no matter how much we give, no matter how many acts of charity we perform, no matter how good we try to be, it will never be enough. We are born in sin, and the only solution to that sin is Jesus.

The gospel tells us that religion is not enough. That God isn't moved by our religious rituals or traditions or even our zeal. What he wants is our complete trust.

Jesus' own words tell us that there is only one way to heaven. That only through him can we find salvation, because he is the only one who has ever dealt with the issue of our rebellion against God. Every religion recognizes that our sin keeps us separated from a holy God, but only Jesus offers us a total solution to the problem.

The gospel tells us that the only way to receive eternal life is to die to self. That only through complete surrender do we find true freedom in Christ.

It's impossible to preach the full counsel of God without offending those who simply don't want to hear it. The gospel message brings us all face-to-face with our own sins and failures, as well as our complete inadequacy to do anything about them on our own.

I've always been a people pleaser by nature, and I often go out of my way to keep from unnecessarily upsetting someone. But when it comes to the gospel message, I'm never willing to compromise. A watered-down version of the truth is not the truth at all. It's simply an attempt to dilute a message that some people find hard to swallow.

That doesn't mean we have to be offensive. Paul encouraged us to speak the truth in love (Eph. 4:15)—to proclaim the gospel boldly and honestly, but always in a spirit of love and compassion and humility.

In his letter to the Colossians, Paul wrote, "Be wise in the way you act toward outsiders; make the most of every opportunity. Let your conversation be always full of grace, seasoned with salt, so that you may know how to answer everyone" (Col. 4:5–6).

The reason I like to share my testimony when witnessing to others is that it creates a common bond. It lets them know that I understand their fears and concerns and that I don't judge them. It tells them that I've been right where they are, and I know how difficult the message of the gospel can be the first time it's heard. I know what it's like to feel confused and powerless and helpless in the face of your own failures and inadequacies. And I know how hard it is to surrender control of your life for the very first time.

The truth of the gospel is a hard and confrontational message. But when shared in the right way and with the right spirit, it can break down the highest walls and soften even the hardest of hearts.

A Life-Changing Truth

I haven't finished telling you what happened with Jim and Nancy.

I awoke from my sleep at 8:00 a.m. to a knock on the door. Jim said he wanted to say good-bye before he had to leave for work. I thanked him for the warm bed and generous hospitality. I could tell something was on his mind.

Just before he left, he said, "You know, Nancy and I stayed up over an hour after you went to bed last night, and we talked about what you had to say. At 3:00 a.m., we both prayed and asked Jesus to come into our hearts. We really want to follow him."

That was the beginning of a long and very special relationship between us. Both of them have been used by God in mighty ways!

The truth of Jesus is an offensive truth, but it's one that every individual needs to hear. Watering the message down to make it more palatable is not an act of kindness. And it's not an option in the eyes of Jesus.

Those who choose to accept it, in spite of the offense, will be forever grateful for your honesty and boldness. Those who don't will at least know you cared enough to try.

11

He Would Be a Friend for Life

By this everyone will know that you are my disciples, if you love one another.

—John 13:35

Christianity is not a religion or a philosophy, but a relationship and a lifestyle.

—Rick Warren

Back in the early nineties, I remember seeing an article in *Sports Illustrated* about a young high school quarterback named Justin Armour. He played for the Manitou Springs Mustangs, a small high school in southern Colorado, and he had just led the team to a state championship. The writer called him a "scholar-athlete who is almost too good to be true."

The article outlined Justin's many high school accomplishments, which included class valedictorian, member of the National Honor Society, president of the student council, editor of the school paper, Bible scholar, and three-sport athlete. His transcript was as long as it was impressive, and every college in the country was courting him.

I remember the article well, because I had heard through the grapevine that he was considering coming to Stanford, and I was hoping to get the chance to meet him. The article also mentioned his strong Christian faith, which got my attention. I asked around and found out when he would be visiting the campus and made a point of watching for him.

The article said he was six feet four inches tall, but he looked even taller the first time I met him. He was a good-looking young man and as polite as anyone I had ever run across. You'd never have known from his humble demeanor that he was one of the best athletes in the country. He and I hit it off immediately, and I told him I'd love the chance to get to know him better if he decided to come to Stanford.

Several months later I learned that he had signed on to play both football and basketball for Stanford. I was thrilled to hear the news, and I couldn't wait to see him again in the fall.

A Lifelong Friend

Justin was recruited by Stanford as a quarterback, but the coach started him from the first game onward as a wide receiver. He could run like a gazelle, and his height gave him a huge advantage on the field. Most cornerbacks couldn't catch him, and they couldn't outreach him even if they did catch him. He was a huge asset to the team.

He and I started meeting together once a week to study the Bible, and we quickly became good friends. It was a nice change for me, meeting with a student who was already in love with Jesus. We had a great time each week digging even deeper into God's Word.

By the time Justin graduated, I considered him one of my very best friends. We had developed an unbreakable bond during his years at Stanford. I try to stay in touch with all the young men I mentor, but in Justin's case it was clear that we had become lifelong friends.

In his senior year, Justin was ranked ninth in the nation for receptions, and second in the Pac-10. He had set the career Stanford school record for receiving yards. He graduated in 1995 and was drafted by the Buffalo Bills.

Throughout his career in the NFL, Justin and I made it a point to stay in touch. After Buffalo, he played for several other teams and even won a Super Bowl ring with the Denver Broncos. He moved around a lot, but we always found time to get together and catch up whenever our schedules allowed.

When Justin got married, he asked me to fly out to Hawaii and perform the ceremony. I had already performed the wedding ceremony for his sister. When his older brother died of a drug overdose, Justin was devastated, and he asked me to come to Colorado for the funeral. Through every major milestone in life, both good and bad, we've been there for each other.

Today Justin lives in Manitou Springs, Colorado, where he runs a Mexican restaurant with his family. He and his wife have two young kids, and they wanted to raise them in a small-town environment with lots of relatives around. He lives a simple life and is still as humble and grounded as any friend I have. I love stopping by to see him whenever I make it to Colorado, just to catch up and see how much his kids have grown.

He once wrote a letter of recommendation for me, and I'm still moved when I think about what he wrote. He said that the reason he decided to attend Stanford as a freshman was because he wanted to be mentored by Jim Stump. He made that decision on his flight home the very day he met me.

Our Deepest Need

You and I are hardwired for relationships. We were created by God to love and to be loved by others. We were created for much more than casual friendships or acquaintances. We need deep and meaningful relationships with those God has put into our lives. We need people who will walk with us through the ups and downs of life, who will be there for us when times get tough, and who will look to us for help and support in their own struggles.

We need people who will intentionally invest in our lives. People who will pray for us when we're sick, counsel us when we're confused, laugh with us when we're happy, defend us when we come under fire, and offer a shoulder to cry on when life gets hard and cumbersome. People who will always be there for us, no matter what. People who need us as much as we need them.

One of the greatest joys I've experienced in my forty-plus years of mentoring is the relationships I've been able to build along the way. I've mentored hundreds of young athletes, and I've remained close friends with just about every one of them. The database on my iPhone is filled with so many names that it's ready to explode. No matter where I travel, I have close friends I can stop and visit with along the way. The Lord has blessed me with many deep and meaningful friendships. Because of that fact, I never feel overwhelmed with the pressures of life. And I never feel alone in my struggles.

Solomon wrote, "Two are better than one, because they have a good return for their labor: If either of them falls down, one can help the other up. But pity anyone who falls and has no one to help them up" (Eccles. 4:9–10).

Meaningful relationships bring us a level of comfort and support that we could never experience on our own. God uses the people around us to help us navigate the scrapes and skirmishes of life. To catch us when we fall, to hold us accountable when we're tempted, to give us a helping hand when we stumble, and to rejoice with us when we overcome.

God himself exists in the comfort of community. The Father, Son, and Holy Spirit are an unbreakable Trinity that defines the perfect relationship. And you and I were created in God's image. We long for community in our lives because the need for relationships is woven into the fabric of our DNA.

When the Pharisees asked Jesus, "Which is the greatest commandment in the Law?" (Matt. 22:36), he answered, "'Love the Lord your God with all your heart and with all your soul and with all your mind.' This is the first and greatest commandment" (vv. 37–38).

But Jesus didn't stop there. He went on to say, "And the second is like it: 'Love your neighbor as yourself'" (v. 39).

We were created first to be in relationship with God, to be in full and perfect communion with Jesus. And from the overflow of our relationship with Christ, we're able to love ourselves properly and to build into the lives of others. When we love God deeply, loving others becomes a natural extension of that relationship.

I've never known anyone who loves God but despises people. It just doesn't work that way. God's love is a well that is constantly overflowing.

Jesus said to his disciples, "As the Father has loved me, so have I loved you. . . . I have called you friends, for everything that I learned from my Father I have made known to you" (John 15:9, 15).

Friendships are the gateway to spiritual community. And community is the avenue through which God draws us into a deeper relationship with himself.

It is also the way he helps us navigate the difficult circumstances of life.

The "C" Word

One day several years ago, I noticed an irregular-looking mole on my abdomen, so I decided to have a dermatologist take a look at it. I went to a nearby office that a family member recommended, and the doctor's response seemed a little strange to me. He said he didn't like the way the mole looked but that we should wait a few months and keep an eye on it.

I tend to trust doctors as a general rule, but something about his approach didn't sit well in my spirit. So I decided to get a second opinion. This time I went to a dermatologist who was referred to me by one of the students I had mentored—a young man who had graduated and was himself one of the most highly recognized physicians in the country. This second dermatologist seemed far more concerned. He took one look at the mole and immediately had his nurse begin prepping me for surgery. The look on his face told me all I needed to know about the urgency of the situation.

He removed the mole, and two days later I got a call from his office saying he wanted to see me again. *That's never a good sign*, I thought.

The day of the appointment, he got right to the point. "Jim, I don't want to worry you, but the lab report showed that your mole was a malignant melanoma. It's the most virulent form of the cancer, and if you hadn't come in when you did, it likely would have metastasized and spread throughout your entire body. You likely wouldn't have lived too much longer."

He went on to explain that he wanted to remove additional tissue and run further tests to make sure they got all the cancerous cells. Obviously I wasn't about to argue.

A Heart at Peace

Thankfully, this doctor found the problem fast enough to fix it, and within a few months I was given a clean bill of health.

I had always wondered how I would react to this type of life-threatening news if it ever came my way. I had spent many hours praying for healing and comfort in the lives of friends and family members, but I'd never been on the business end of those prayers. At least not with something as menacing as cancer.

My response was exactly what I had always hoped it would be. It was not one of dread or fear or even panic. In fact, it was the exact opposite. Through the entire ordeal, I felt completely calm and at peace. I never once found myself angry with God or questioning his will. I never wondered, *Why me?* or *What have I done to deserve this?* And I never doubted that God was in complete control. I've never considered myself super spiritual, but I have walked with Jesus long enough to know that he does not make mistakes, and I trust him.

Between doctor visits, there were long stretches of time when I found myself in medical limbo, waiting for test results to come back from the lab, and during those times I felt completely at peace with whatever the news would be.

I remember praying once, *Lord, if you want to take me home to heaven, I'm ready to go. You've allowed me to live a life far fuller and more rewarding than I could have ever dreamed. I have a wonderful wife and three beautiful children who are all walking faithfully with you. And I have hundreds of spiritual children I get to spend eternity with in heaven. I have a lot more I want to accomplish for your kingdom, but if it's my time to go, I'm completely ready. Thank you, Lord, for the wonderful life you've given me.*

I never once remember lying awake at night worrying or dreading a call from the doctor. I had no idea what the future held or what the next series of tests would reveal, but I trusted God entirely to get me through everything.

I was hanging out one day on the sidelines during practice when one of the Stanford coaches called out to me. He was a man with whom I'd had very little contact through the years. He said to me, "Jim, I just heard this afternoon what you've been going through, and I'm really concerned for you. How are you handling everything?"

I said to him, "You know, ever since the doctor told me I had cancer, I've been completely at peace. I know I'm in God's hands, so I'm not worried at all. But thanks for your concern."

His response completely floored me. "That really doesn't surprise me," he said. "I've been watching you the past two hours since I heard the news, and I can't believe how well you seem to be handling it. If something like this happened to me, I'd be a basket case. I don't know how you can be at such peace, but I wish I had your courage."

I smiled and explained to him that it was my relationship with Jesus that gave me the strength to get through tough times. He asked me if I could come to his office after practice and talk with him further.

Later that afternoon, while sitting in his office, the two of us prayed as he asked Jesus to come into his heart and be his Lord and Savior.

It was another simple but stark reminder to me how readily God can use our modest acts of faith and trust for his greater glory.

The Beauty of Friends

I learned two important lessons during that time of my life.

The first is, when it comes to your health, never be too proud to get a second opinion. Doctors are great allies to have during times of sickness, and they take their jobs very seriously, but they're still just human, and sometimes they get it wrong.

The second is, when life gets confusing, don't be afraid to lean on the friends God has put in your life.

I'm convinced that the main reason I was able to be at such peace during a difficult time was the good friends who surrounded me on every side. I shared my news with only a few trusted friends, but within days I had dozens of people praying on my behalf, sending me words of encouragement, giving me support and reassurance that everything was going to be all right. I can't remember the last time I felt so loved and appreciated. At every turn, people were asking what they could do to help and going out of their way to let me know how much they cared. Often they would lay hands on me and pray for healing, and each time I felt the Holy Spirit's strength flowing through my heart and body.

Had I been on my own, without deep and meaningful friendships in my life, I honestly don't know how I would have handled the news. But because of the many loyal relationships that God brought to my aid, the disease became more a source of strength and faith than a test of conviction.

That's what solid, godly relationships do for us. They create a support system that can help us navigate even the darkest hours of life. They become the angels of mercy and ministry that God uses to bring us comfort in times of need.

During my bout with cancer, it seems that I was the only one who wasn't worried about my health. And there was something profoundly moving and reassuring about that fact.

A Living Gospel

One of the last admonitions Jesus gave his disciples before going to the cross was, "As I have loved you, so you must love one another. By this everyone will know that you are my disciples, if you love one another" (John 13:34–35).

You and I live in a world that craves relationships. People long to be loved and understood. We need the comfort of community, and in the deepest recesses of our hearts, we all know that this is our greatest need, even if we don't quite know how to articulate it. We long to be in relationship with God and to be surrounded by friends who love us. And this is the need that Christian community fills in a way that no other group can.

Sharing our faith with others is about so much more than telling people about Jesus. It's about opening up our hearts and lives and letting them in. It's about becoming the avenue through which God can show them his love and kindness. It's about putting skin on the gospel message so that people can see and touch it firsthand.

It's about developing intentional friendships with those who need Jesus so that we can show them what a true relationship with Christ looks like.

Jesus offers us more than salvation; he promises to become a friend not only in this life but for eternity. And who among us could possibly refuse an offer like that?

PART 3

Simple Steps
to Sharing Your Faith

Remember that mentor leadership is all about serving.

—Tony Dungy

While the trend of the Church to focus on social justice is great—and the trend to focus on spiritual formation is wonderful—I fear that reaching a lost world is being marginalized further and further. I fear that the Church continues to slip in its core mission of evangelism.

—Bill Hybels

The greatest form of praise is the sound of consecrated feet seeking out the lost and helpless.

—Billy Graham

12

The Indescribable Gospel of Grace

My deepest awareness of myself is that I am deeply loved by Jesus Christ and I have done nothing to earn it or deserve it.

—Brennan Manning, *The Ragamuffin Gospel*

Robert came to Stanford as the number one–ranked tennis player in the country. And he had no use for spiritual matters. Tennis was his entire life, and anything else was just a distraction from the thing he loved most. I ran across him frequently since I spent a lot of time around the tennis team, but he always kept his distance.

A number of the Stanford tennis players had come to faith in Jesus, and several of them were meeting with me once a week, so I began hosting a regular Bible study with the team. And each time we met, all the players would show up, including Robert. The tennis team was a tight-knit group, and they did everything together. Robert would almost always be there, but he seldom spoke and never acknowledged anything that was said. He just sat in the back of the room, checking his watch every five or ten minutes.

I had given every player on the team a nice Bible with their name inscribed on the cover, but Robert never picked his up, so I decided one day to hand-deliver it to his dorm room. I thought it might give me an opportunity to reach out to him or answer any questions he might have.

I found his room and knocked on the door. I could tell the minute he opened it that he wasn't happy to see me. He didn't even invite me in; he just stood in the doorway, probably wondering why I was there.

"I gave a copy of the Bible to all the players and noticed that you hadn't picked yours up yet, so I thought I would bring it by," I said, trying to sound as pleasant as possible.

He took the Bible from my hand and, without looking at it, threw it into the far corner of his room. It was obvious he had no interest in talking, so I made polite conversation for a few seconds and then slowly backed away from the door. He quickly closed it, and I went on my way, wondering if I'd ever get another chance to reach out to him.

I had little personal contact with Robert over the next three years. He still showed up at our Bible studies, but only because the rest of his team was there. I would pass him in the student union from time to time, but he never looked in my direction.

Toward the end of Robert's junior year, he decided to turn pro and make his living on the growing tennis circuit. One day, out of the blue, I received a letter from him in the mail. I was shocked to see his name on the return address. I had followed his successful young career and knew that he was traveling to tournaments around the globe. In the letter he was writing from a plane on his way from New Zealand to Australia, he told me where he would be playing in another tennis tournament, and he had a favor to ask of me. He had just gotten engaged to his girlfriend, and he suddenly found himself worried about their future. "I've started to realize that we don't have a snowball's chance in hell of surviving this marriage unless we have something more to base it on than love," he wrote.

He also told me that he had been reading the Bible I gave him and had been looking for advice on marriage, but he couldn't find anything specific. He added, "I'm writing to ask if you'd be willing to get together with me when I get home so we can talk about it."

It was a nice surprise for me, and I couldn't wait to see him when he got back to Stanford.

The Good News of Jesus

A few days after he returned to the Bay Area, Robert and I met for lunch. I was surprised by how pleasant and friendly he had become. The only thing he brought was the Bible I had given him three years earlier—the one he had thrown into the corner of his dorm room. He laid it on the table in front of him when he sat down.

I congratulated him on his engagement and we made small talk for a few minutes, and then I said to him, "You know, Robert, the Bible has a lot of good advice on marriage, and I want to study that with you. But quite honestly, there's not much point in talking about having a Christian marriage until you first understand what it means to be a Christian. Can I start by telling you about Jesus?"

For the first time since I had known Robert, I got the opportunity to share the Good News of Jesus with him. As I told him the story of the cross, and how Jesus died for our sins then rose from the grave three days later, Robert sat wide-eyed and fascinated, as if he'd never before heard the story. I couldn't believe this was the same person who had seemed so uninterested in even engaging in conversation for the last three years.

By the time I finished sharing the Good News with him, Robert was ready to commit his life to Jesus. So we bowed our heads as he asked Jesus to become his Lord and Savior.

"This is the greatest thing I've ever heard," he said as we finished praying. "Can you tell my fiancée about this?"

The next evening the three of us had dinner together, and afterward we visited over coffee as I shared the story of Jesus with her as well. Her name was Bella, and she was a beautiful and perceptive young woman. She, too, committed her life to Jesus after hearing the Good News.

It's always a joyous occasion when someone decides to become a follower of Jesus, and I never get tired of praying with people for the first time as they accept him as their Lord and Savior, but there was something about this moment that was especially moving to me. As the three of us prayed at the table that evening, I fought back tears as I thought of the eternal implications of this particular event.

Here were two people who had committed to spending the rest of their lives together, and now they were committing to giving their lives to God as well. They would be entering into marriage with an entirely new understanding of the covenant they were making, as well as God's desire for their relationship. It was a miraculous moment, as tender and touching as any I'd ever experienced. I thank God that he allowed me to play a small role in drawing Robert and Bella into his eternal embrace.

Transforming Grace

Robert and I continued to meet whenever he was in town between tournaments over the next few months, and we began studying the biblical principles of marriage. Often Bella would join us, and I had a great time getting to know them as a couple. I could literally see the change in their lives as the Holy Spirit began shaping and molding them from the inside out. Everything about them began to transform—their speech, their demeanor, even the way they treated each other. God was clearly working in their lives.

Then one day I got a call from Robert's younger brother, Gavin. Gavin was also a world-class tennis player and an integral member of the Stanford team. In fact, he and Robert were the first blood brothers to ever be ranked in the top ten in the world in both singles and doubles.

The minute I picked up the phone, I could sense in Gavin's voice that he was irritated with me. "What have you done with Robert and Bella?" he asked.

"What do you mean?" I responded.

"I'm just wondering what you've done with them. I was at a party with them last night, and they were completely different than I'd ever seen them. They were actually being nice to people—including me! And that's not the Robert I know."

I sensed that Gavin's real concern wasn't how "nice" Robert was acting, but whether he had lost his competitive edge.

He told me he confronted them at the party about their new demeanor, asking them why they were acting so different. "They told me I needed to ask Stumper about it," he said, "so that's why I decided to call you. Is there something I need to know?"

I assured him that everything was fine with Robert and Bella. "They're still the same people, but now they have a personal relationship with Jesus, and that has made a significant difference."

I waited for him to respond but heard only silence. "What about you?" I asked him. "Have you ever explored the teachings of Jesus? If not, I'd love to meet with you tomorrow and discuss this further."

Again there was a long pause. Reluctantly, he agreed to meet with me.

Gavin was as skeptical as any nonbeliever I'd ever studied with. No matter what truth of Scripture I brought up, he'd immediately question it. It was obvious that he'd spent a lot of time reading material that refuted the claims of Jesus, but almost no time actually looking at the evidence to support those claims. Over the next three months, we met each week to study, and during that time he conducted the most comprehensive investigation of Scripture I'd ever witnessed. He devoured the books I recommended, and he personally interviewed the guys on the football team who were meeting with me to find out what had motivated them to commit their lives to Jesus. It made for an exhausting experience, but I patiently answered every question he threw my way because I could tell he had become a legitimate seeker after truth.

Finally, after months of doubt and research, Gavin raised the white flag of surrender. He could no longer deny the truth of Jesus' life and death and resurrection. So one day he came to my table in the Sports Café and told me he was ready to commit his life to God and become a follower of Jesus.

A Family Miracle

Robert and Gavin had grown up in Southern California, and their father was one of the leading tennis-teaching professionals in the country, which explained why they had both been raised on the tennis court.

Later that spring the two of them headed home to train for some upcoming tournaments, and about a month later I received a call from their father. In his own very direct way he asked me, "Jim, what have you done with my two boys?"

"I'm not sure what you mean," I answered.

"Ever since they've been here, they've been completely different people. They're actually being nice to each other and respectful toward me. It's not that I don't like it, it's just that they've never been this way before. So I asked them what was going on, and they told me I needed to talk to you to find out."

I couldn't help but smile as he talked, and I almost started laughing. "I'd love the chance to talk to you about it," I said.

He told me he would be flying to the Bay Area the next day to sit down with me for lunch and find out what was going on.

He was a gruff man, with a larger-than-life personality and a thunderous laugh. We had a great time conversing over lunch, and I shared the gospel message with him. He had already witnessed God's transforming power in the lives of his two sons, so he was extremely open to hearing more about Jesus. By the end of the lunch, he told me that he'd like to accept Jesus as his Lord, so we prayed together.

I knew of a good church in his hometown, so I arranged for him to meet the pastor when he returned home. He immediately plugged into the church and became one of their most consistent members. After a year of faithful involvement, he took on the role of visiting each new person who showed up at the church and made sure they knew how to become a follower of Jesus. It seemed like each week he would call me with another story of someone coming to faith in Jesus. Over his remaining years, he led scores of people to the Lord.

Though Robert, Gavin, and their father have had their challenges like we all do, the Lord has done an amazing miracle in the life of this great family, and I'm thrilled to be able to call them friends. Several years ago, a national sports magazine ran a feature article on Robert and Gavin, and I was honored that they mentioned me in the interview as a key friend and mentor during their years at Stanford. Their kind words touched me deeply.

The Gospel of Grace

The word *gospel* literally means "good news," but I consider that to be the greatest understatement of all time. The gospel is incredible news! It's a kind of news that's beyond human explanation. It's phenomenal news! It's unbelievable news! It's extraordinary news! It is incomprehensible news!

You could wear out a thesaurus trying to describe it and never quite get it right.

The Good News of Jesus is a message that defies logic. It redefines everything you and I have ever thought to be true about life on earth, and it brings an eternal perspective that changes everything about us.

The Good News tells us that you and I have an opportunity to live in direct relationship with the God of the universe—the God who created the world and everything in it—and that our relationship with God forever changes the course of our eternal future. More than that, it brings transforming power into our lives here on earth.

In Matthew's Gospel, Jesus described our relationship with God as a treasure hidden in a field and a pearl of great value (13:44, 45). Peter tells us, "Even angels long to look into these things" (1 Pet. 1:12).

Salvation is a gift from God that no one can earn but everyone can have. And it is the only gift in the universe that comes with no strings attached, no hidden agenda, no preconditions. God longs to be in relationship with us, and through the blood of Jesus on the cross, he built a bridge between his world and ours. All we have to do is accept his free offer and walk across that bridge.

If that isn't good news, I don't know what is!

This is a message worth savoring. It's an offer worth embracing. And it's good news worth sharing with anyone willing to give us a few minutes of their time.

When I think back to the day I had the opportunity to share the Good News of Jesus with Robert for the first time, I'm reminded all over again of what a remarkable, life-changing message we have. The story was unlike anything he had ever heard or imagined, and he sat in wide-eyed wonder the entire time. And I'll never forget the words he uttered after praying to accept Jesus into his life: "This is the greatest thing I've ever heard."

And that is not an exaggeration. There is no news on earth greater than the Good News of Jesus. There is no name in heaven or on earth that compares. Jesus is everything, and everything hinges on the person of Jesus.

The gospel is God's most significant message to mankind, and he gave it to us written in the blood of his only Son. How could we possibly keep such an indescribable truth to ourselves?

The late author Brennan Manning summed it up better than I ever could: "My friends, if this is not good news to you, you have never understood the gospel of grace."[6]

13

Would You Like to Know God Personally?

As you love God and serve him, you will undoubtedly experience the greatest adventure life has to offer.

—Dr. Bill Bright

'm not sure why I was fortunate enough to win the "job lottery," but I'm sure glad I did. I can't imagine spending my days doing anything other than telling people about Jesus.

For the past forty-plus years I've had the joy of meeting and mentoring some of the greatest young athletes in the country, and every one of them holds a special place in my heart. I've made more good friends than any one person should be allowed to have.

Today, I meet with about thirty-five student athletes each quarter for an hour each week for a time of prayer and study, and almost every one of them had no concept of a relationship with Jesus when we first met. They are all bright and promising young men, many of whom came to Stanford on an athletic scholarship, usually with academic honors. Yet for one reason or another, they had never heard and accepted the truth of Jesus.

Most people find that hard to believe, but it's true. Even in the United States, many people live their entire lives never hearing the Good News that God loves them and wants a personal relationship with them. Everyone has heard about religion and the church, but that's a far cry from actually being introduced to the true person of Jesus and the eternal relationship God offers.

Throughout my career as a spiritual mentor, I've used a very simple tool to help walk people through the steps of developing a meaningful relationship with Jesus. It's the little booklet I've referred to a number of times in earlier chapters. It was written many years ago by Dr. Bill Bright and originally published under the title *Have You Heard of the Four Spiritual Laws?* It has been redesigned to communicate better with this generation, and it is now being reprinted under the title *Would You Like to Know God Personally?*

I've seen a lot of different books and pamphlets through the years that were designed to help introduce people to Jesus, but I've never found one quite as simple and effective as this small, sixteen-page booklet. I encourage anyone interested in sharing their faith with others to pick up a few copies and keep them on hand.

For those who have never walked someone through the steps to finding eternal life, let's take a little time to examine these principles a bit deeper. Let me walk with you through the steps I use each time I sit down with someone who has never heard and accepted the Good News of Jesus. These timeless principles are taken directly from Bill Bright's book *Would You Like to Know God Personally?*

This isn't the only way to share your faith, and it may not even be the best way, but it has worked well for me.

Principle #1: *God loves you and created you to know him personally. He has a wonderful plan for your life.*

Perhaps the most well-known passage in all of Scripture is John 3:16: "For God so loved the world that he gave his one and only Son, that whoever believes in him shall not perish but have eternal life."

It's a passage that almost every person I've talked to has heard at one time or another—even those who have never owned or read a Bible. It's impossible to watch a football or soccer game without seeing someone hoisting a huge sign with "3:16" on it. It's the most universally quoted passage in the entire Bible, and there's good reason for that.

John 3:16 sums up the message of the gospel better than any other sentence in Scripture. It's a simple and succinct passage that explains exactly who Jesus is, why he came, and what his life, death, and resurrection mean for us all.

Jesus is God's only Son, and he came to earth with the express purpose of laying down his life on our behalf and forgiving our sins. Because of this, you and I can escape death and have eternal life with him in heaven. All we have to do is believe and accept his offer.

Jesus is the living, breathing expression of God's love for us. And because of his great love, he created a way for each of us to live with him in heaven for eternity.

But Jesus offers more than eternal life in heaven. He offers a full and joyous life on earth. In John 10:10, he tells us, "I have come that [you] may have life, and have it to the full."

When we accept God's free offer of salvation, he promises to walk with us daily. To be not only our Savior but a personal friend. When we pray, he hears us. When we hurt, he comforts us. When we're happy, he rejoices with us. When we're sad, he wipes away the tears. God becomes a real and integral part of our lives. We call him Father, and he calls us his children.

God longs to have a deep and personal relationship with each one of us. This was his purpose from the beginning of creation, and it is his perfect plan for our lives. We were created to be in relationship with God, and through Jesus, we each have an opportunity to fully embrace that relationship.

But if that's true, why haven't more people found and accepted this relationship? Why is there so much confusion and animosity toward God?

In the Garden of Gethsemane, the night before his crucifixion, Jesus prayed, "Now this is eternal life: that they know you, the only true God, and Jesus Christ, whom you have sent" (John 17:3).

Jesus prayed that all of us would find eternal life through his death and resurrection, but even as the words left his lips, he knew that many would not. Some would be cold and apathetic, and others would even reject God's invitation. Jesus knew that there was a reality in the world that even the most sacrificial act could not overcome.

Something in the world is keeping us apart. Something is standing in the way, keeping men and women from hearing and accepting the news of God's incomprehensible grace. And the second principle explains what that something is.

Principle #2: *People are sinful and separated from God, so we cannot know him personally or experience his love and plan.*

The apostle Paul wrote, "For all have sinned and fall short of the glory of God" (Rom. 3:23).

Sin may very well be the most misunderstood word on the planet. If you were to ask a hundred people to list those sins that separate us from God, most would likely begin with the things that we all know are wrong, like murder, adultery, and stealing—the obvious sins that "good" people would never commit.

But God's view of sin is completely different.

In his first recorded sermon on a mountainside near the Sea of Galilee, Jesus said to the crowd, "You have heard that it was said to the people long ago, 'You shall not murder, and anyone who murders will be subject to judgment.' But I tell you that anyone who is angry with a brother or sister will be subject to judgment" (Matt. 5:21–22).

For thousands of years, the people of Israel had been struggling to keep God's laws, and suddenly God came to earth in the flesh to explain that keeping the spirit of the law is just as important as keeping the letter of it. Jesus was saying to them, "It isn't just the act of murder that separates you from God; it's the attitude behind it. Just desiring to do wrong is sinful."

Jesus went on to say, "You have heard that it was said, 'You shall not commit adultery.' But I tell you that anyone who looks at a woman lustfully has already committed adultery with her in his heart" (vv. 27–28).

And who in the crowd could possibly say they had never lusted? You and I can't say that either. In God's eyes, just imagining an act of sin is the same as committing it. Just wanting to do something disobedient is disobedience to God! Who among us could possibly live up to that kind of standard?

The answer is simple. We can't. None of us can escape the influence of sin. We all fall short.

You and I were created to be in perfect fellowship with God, but we were also created with a will of our own. We have the ability to accept God's plan for our life, but we also have the ability to reject it. God loves us deeply, but he doesn't force us to love him. No matter how good we've tried to be or how good we think we are, we have all sinned against God. And that creates a huge problem for us, because, as Paul tells us, "The wages of sin is death" (Rom. 6:23).

You and I are more than physical beings; we also have a soul. And when we die, our soul separates from our body. Our body may be laid in the ground to turn to dust, but our soul doesn't go there with it. Yet that soul has to go somewhere.

That's what heaven was created for. Our soul was intended to live with God for eternity. But heaven is God's home, a holy and consecrated place, and he can't allow it to be corrupted by sin. Sin creates a chasm between us and God—a chasm that we could never hope to cross on our own.

I often ask people to imagine what would happen if the world's greatest long jumper announced one day that he was planning to jump across the Grand Canyon. On the day of the event, huge crowds gather to watch him try, with every news station in the country there to capture the feat on film.

He sets up for his jump and starts running toward the canyon with lightning speed. Just as he reaches the edge, he jumps for all he is worth. No human has ever run this fast or leaped with this kind of momentum. He shatters the all-time world record, jumping farther than anyone thought humanly possible. The judges estimate the distance at a staggering sixty feet, more than twice the length of any jump in history.

By every standard this would be an amazing accomplishment, but it's still far shy of the eighteen miles needed to reach the other side. The applause quickly dies down to a whisper as the jumper plunges to his death at the bottom of the canyon.

That's what it's like when you and I try to find heaven on our own merit. It can't be done, no matter how far we think we can jump. Sin is the gravity that weighs on our soul and keeps us from reaching the other side on our own power.

And since you and I could never hope to bridge this chasm on our own, God built a bridge for us.

Principle #3: *Jesus Christ is God's only provision for our sin. Through him alone we can know God personally and experience God's love and plan.*

Paul wrote, "God demonstrates his own love for us in this: While we were still sinners, Christ died for us" (Rom. 5:8).

Sin has consequences. And it has to be dealt with. If the wages of sin is spiritual death, then someone has to die in order to pay for our sins. That's what Jesus came into the world to do.

Jesus went to the cross to pay the penalty for our sins and bridge the chasm between God and us. When Jesus walked the earth, he clearly displayed his power over the natural world. The miracles he performed are documented historical facts. With just a touch of his hand he was able to heal the sick, cure the lame and crippled, bring sight to the blind, even raise people from the dead. He could have easily avoided his own capture and crucifixion at the hands of the Roman soldiers, but he chose not to. He willingly laid down his life on the cross, because he knew that it was the only way to bring you and me back into relationship with God.

Paul wrote, "Christ died for our sins. . . . He was buried. . . . He was raised on the third day according to the Scriptures. . . . He appeared to Cephas, and then to the Twelve. After that, he appeared to more than five hundred" (1 Cor. 15:3–6).

If the story of Jesus had ended at his death, then you and I might never have heard of him. His teachings would have been nothing more than another set of codes or ethics to live by. He would be no different than any other self-proclaimed prophet, peddling his brand of religion to anyone who might be listening.

But that isn't what happened. His life didn't end at his crucifixion. After three days in the grave, Jesus rose from death and walked out of the tomb, just as he said he would. And more than five hundred people at one time saw him alive after his resurrection.

The reason you and I are able to have a deep and personal relationship with Jesus is because he is still alive. He conquered death on our behalf, and now he lives once again in eternal fellowship with his Father. He built a bridge to heaven and is waiting there for you and me to join him.

Jesus made one of the most amazing claims ever uttered when he said, "I am the way and the truth and the life. No one comes to the Father except through me" (John 14:6).

However, just because someone took the time and effort to build a bridge doesn't mean you and I are forced to cross it. Jesus opened up a pathway for us to be reunited with God forever, but whether we walk that path is entirely up to us. We still have free will. God longs to be in relationship with us, but he doesn't force himself on us. You and I have to willingly accept God's offer of an eternal relationship. And the only way to do that is through Jesus.

When I was a young believer fresh out of college, my spiritual mentor told me a story that had a huge impact on my life and really brought this concept to life for me. It was a true story that happened many years ago. A man had committed a crime and was sentenced to death, but shortly before he was to be executed, President Andrew Jackson pardoned him. The warden brought the pardon to him in his cell and said, "Congratulations, here is your pardon. You are free to go."

To the warden's surprise, the man refused to leave. "I do not want the pardon," he said.

Not knowing what to do, the warden took the case to court. Eventually the case ended up before the Supreme Court under the title *United States v. Wilson*. The court eventually ruled that a pardon was not valid unless it was accepted, and soon afterward the prisoner was executed.

In the same way, Jesus, the ultimate purveyor of justice, has pardoned us from our sins and paid the penalty on our behalf.

We've been given complete absolution from our transgressions. But his pardon is not valid unless you and I accept it.

Principle #4: *We must individually receive Jesus Christ as Savior and Lord; then we can know God personally and experience his love and plan.*

John wrote, "To all who did receive him, to those who believed in his name, he gave the right to become children of God" (John 1:12).

When we accept God's gift of eternal salvation, we become more than participants in his grace; we become his children, heirs to all he has to offer. We are grafted into the family of God. And being a child of God, instead of a servant, brings an entirely new dynamic to the relationship. Because we're adopted children, all of our debts—both past and future ones—are completely covered. We come into the family debt-free and forgiven, and God assumes responsibility for our future. We become God's personal concern, and he takes a vested interest in our lives. Every blessing he has to offer becomes ours.

Paul tells us, "It is by grace you have been saved, through faith— and this is not from yourselves, it is the gift of God—not by works, so that no one can boast" (Eph. 2:8–9).

Our inheritance into God's family is a gift that we could never imagine earning on our own. There is nothing we could possibly do to deserve such an incredible birthright. Grace is a free gift from God, and it comes only when we humble ourselves before him and accept his pardon. We bring nothing to the relationship and have nothing to offer but spiritual and emotional surrender.

To those of us willing to open our hands and our hearts to God and accept this free gift of grace, Jesus says, "Here I am! I stand at the door and knock. If anyone hears my voice and opens the door, I will come in and eat with that person, and they with me" (Rev. 3:20).

Jesus is ready and willing to come into our lives and bring us into his eternal family, and he even stands knocking on the door of our hearts in order to get our attention. He longs to come in and engage us in the relationship. But he won't come in uninvited. You and I have to open the door and let him in. We have to willfully accept him as our Lord and Savior.

Coming to Jesus is not just an intellectual exercise or an emotional experience. And just believing that Jesus is God's Son is not enough. Even Satan knows that to be true.

It's a conscious and willful decision of the heart to surrender our lives over to God's will. It is you and me deciding once and for all that we could never earn God's grace and acceptance on our own, humbly coming to God with open hands and open hearts, and thanking him for forgiving us for the things we've done and accepting us as children of his grace.

So What Now?

So what happens when you decide to accept God's free offer of eternal salvation?

That's a question that comes up often when I share the Good News with people. And often I answer with a simple illustration.

When I was courting my wife, Linda, there came a point in our relationship when we both decided to make a permanent commitment to each other. We wanted to spend the rest of our lives together, and we instinctively knew that such a permanent covenant required more than good intentions. What we needed was a public declaration of our pledge. So we planned a wedding ceremony, where we openly expressed our covenantal pledge before God and others.

It doesn't take a ceremony to accept Jesus as your Lord, but it does require an open expression of the covenantal commitment.

You accept Jesus with your heart, and then you seal the covenant by expressing your commitment in prayer.

There are no set words to speak and no hidden formula. Just speak to God from your heart, asking him to come into your life and become your Lord and Savior.

If you've never prayed before or are unsure what to say, here is a simple prayer to get you started.

Lord Jesus, I need you. Thank you for dying on the cross for my sins. I open the door of my life and receive you as my Savior and Lord. Thank you for forgiving my sins and giving me eternal life. Take control of the throne of my life. Make me the kind of person you want me to be.

Then I would encourage you to take a step of faith like I did and thank Jesus for coming into your life and hearing your prayer as he promised.

Many people find it hard to believe that such a simple prayer could bring about life-altering change and significance. But in God's economy, prayer is a powerful and miraculous thing. Even the simplest act of faith on our part can mobilize God to move mountains.

When you humble yourself before God and pray a prayer of faith for the first time, expressing your desire to surrender your life to his will, he hears and answers your prayer. You can be certain that he will accept you into his family and come into your life, just as he promised he would.

Finding Your Own Approach

There is no secret formula or format for sharing your faith with others, but it's always a good idea to have some kind of road map to keep you heading in the right direction. And that's what these principles from the booklet *Would You Like to Know God Personally?* are designed to do. Using these four principles as your outline is a good approach to keeping your thoughts on track and your words on topic.

I always like to give the person with whom I am meeting a copy of the booklet so they can refer back to it for themselves. It also gives them something they can use when sharing their faith with other family members and friends who are interested.

But the best way to share your faith is to share yourself. To simply talk about your story and what first brought you to faith in Jesus. People can argue with your words, but no one can argue with your story. So talk about your relationship with God. Discuss what it was that brought you to the point of inviting him into your life, how you did so, and what that relationship has done for your future. And be specific about the changes that have come about in your life. The tendency is to use glittering generalities, but people are interested in the practical ways your relationship with Jesus has affected your life.

You might also take time to memorize those key verses in Scripture that lead people toward a relationship with Jesus, beginning with the ones in this chapter. Maybe even highlight them in your Bible and bookmark the pages so you can readily find them.

But the most important thing to remember when sharing your faith is that you are not alone. Jesus said, "Where two or three gather in my name, there am I with them" (Matt. 18:20). Anytime you share Jesus with a friend, you can be sure that the Holy Spirit is right there with you, guiding your thoughts and directing your words.

I know that God is a relentless pursuer of hearts, and because of that, anytime I have an opportunity to share Jesus with another person, I assume that the Holy Spirit has already been working in their life, softening their heart and drawing them toward himself. More often than not, that assumption proves to be right on target.

I'm continually amazed by how many people are ready to accept Jesus as their Lord once they hear who he really is and the eternal relationship he offers. It may be my words they hear, but I'm not naïve enough to think that I'm the one who led them to faith or convinced them to surrender. The voice they hear in their spirit is the voice of God, urging them to stop running, to stop wandering, to stop doubting, and to start believing what they know in their hearts to be true. He's beckoning them to come home, where they belong.

14

It's All about Jesus

For what I received I passed on to you as of first importance: that Christ died for our sins according to the Scriptures, that he was buried, that he was raised on the third day according to the Scriptures.

—The apostle Paul (1 Cor. 15:3–4)

Many years ago, while working with Campus Crusade at Reading University, I was sitting in the student union enjoying a hot cup of afternoon tea. It was a typically cold, blustery winter day in England, and the union was bustling with students escaping the bitter afternoon chill.

A young student sat down next to me, and the two of us struck up a friendly conversation. After finding out that I was an American, he asked, "So what brings you to England?"

"I'm here talking with students about how they can have a personal relationship with Jesus," I explained.

A bemused look came across his face, and suddenly the tone of our conversation completely changed. He gulped down the last of his tea and said, "I can't stay right now, but I'd be very interested in talking to you about this later this afternoon. I have some friends I'm sure would like to ask you some questions too. Will you be around in about three hours?"

I smiled and assured him I would be there as he quickly gathered his things and hurried away. I assumed he was simply late to class, but something about his behavior seemed strange to me. I began to wonder what I had just gotten myself into.

A close friend was in town visiting with me at the time, so the two of us got together for a time of prayer before my afternoon meeting with the young student. Then just before 3:00 p.m., the two of us made our way back to the student union to wait for him. I was still a bit apprehensive.

A Royal Setup

Sure enough, the young student showed up right on time, and he wasn't alone. He had about twenty friends following closely behind him as he sauntered in our direction. He had a cocky grin on his face as he invited us to a room down the hall. He took a seat across from me, and about ten of his friends grabbed chairs and gathered them in a large circle. The rest of the group found seats behind them. I felt like I was the focus of some kind of mass intervention, being confronted by a roomful of people I'd never met.

He introduced their group as the official Reading University Atheist Club, and himself as the president. Then he said to his friends, "Jim has promised to answer every question we have about God."

Of course, I had made no such promise, but I didn't feel it was the time to quibble.

One by one, his friends began pelting me with questions about God and Jesus and philosophy and the Christian faith. With each question, I'd do my best to thoughtfully answer, but before I'd have a chance to finish, another question would come my way. And none of them were really questions, but rather attempts to stump me and make my beliefs look stupid.

One person would bring up an obscure passage from the Bible that he believed was inconsistent with another teaching, then say to me, "How do you explain that?" The cheering section behind him would sneer and clap in amusement. Then before I could open my mouth, another person would bring up some perceived flaw in the Christian belief system. I quickly realized what an exercise in futility it would be to try to answer, so I bit my tongue and waited for a chance to speak.

Finally, after most had had their chance to talk, I signaled a time-out, and when the voices died down, I said to them, "Pardon me, but I don't think you people are even coming close to the real issue with your questions."

Several leaned back in their chairs with raised eyebrows. Then one person ventured to ask, "Okay, so what is the issue as you see it?"

I answered, "The question you need to be asking is, 'How do we deal with the resurrection of Jesus Christ?' Because everything about the Christian faith hinges on the claims of Jesus. If Jesus truly rose from the dead, that fact holds tremendous consequences for us, because no man has ever done that before. If he conquered death, it means that he is who he said and that he is still alive today. If he didn't rise from the dead, then Christianity is nothing more than a good set of principles to live by. So if you really want to discredit the Christian faith, all you have to do is prove that the resurrection didn't happen. And that's a pretty easy thing to examine."

I paused to let my words sink in. I could tell they were taken off guard by my premise.

"If you're really interested," I continued, "I'm happy to examine the evidence with you. But if not, we're all just wasting our time, and I have a lot of other things I could be doing."

There was a long pause before a few of the more vocal members of the group nodded in agreement, so I got comfortable in my chair and began outlining the resurrection story as the Bible recorded it.

I knew I was in for a long afternoon, so I silently prayed for wisdom as I set out to explore and defend the claims of Jesus.

Staying on Point

One of the most important things I've learned through years of sharing my faith is that people who don't know Jesus have seldom taken the time to actually investigate his teachings. And much of what they think about the Christian faith is based more on misconception than reality.

Most people I meet don't claim to be atheists; they simply haven't thought much about what they really believe. And those who do say they are atheists are almost always basing their disbelief on some perceived error or inconsistency they've heard about. They will often say they have studied the Scriptures at length, when what they've really done is read books and articles from hardened skeptics, most of whom take a completely dishonest approach to Scripture in order to discredit it.

A large number of the people with whom I have spoken have initially based their beliefs more on emotion than thoughtful examination. And because of that fact, it is important when sharing your faith with a friend to keep them on topic. Everyone has preconceived notions about God and religion, and conversations can quickly turn into a futile exercise in rabbit chasing.

I've shared my faith with literally thousands of people through the years, and when I was young in my walk I went down more dead-end trails than I care to admit. However, I've learned that the only way to truly keep the conversation on point is to focus on the person of Jesus and how one begins a personal relationship with him. If the claims of Jesus don't hold water, nothing about our faith is worth sharing. But if they do, there's no more significant truth in the universe.

It truly is all about Jesus.

The apostle Paul succinctly summed up the whole of the gospel message in his letter to the Colossian church.

> The Son is the image of the invisible God, the firstborn over all creation. For in him all things were created: things in heaven and on earth, visible and invisible, whether thrones or powers or rulers or authorities; all things have been created through him and for him. He is before all things, and in him all things hold together. And he is the head of the body, the church; he is the beginning and the firstborn from among the dead, so that in everything he might have the supremacy. For God was pleased to have all his fullness dwell in him, and through him to reconcile to himself all things, whether things on earth or things in heaven, by making peace through his blood, shed on the cross. (Col. 1:15–20)

Paul understood a truth more powerful and significant than all other truths combined: Jesus is the center of all, and everything in creation revolves around him. He is the image of God, the firstborn of all creation. And everything was created through him, by him, and for him. He is the beginning and the end, the fullness of God that holds everything together. Through his blood on the cross, all things in heaven and earth were reconciled to God. Jesus is not just another belief system; he is the centerpiece of the universe, the cornerstone of all creation, the foundation of humanity.

Either Jesus is God in the flesh, or he is the greatest hoax ever perpetrated on the world. And because of that, any meaningful discussion about the Christian faith has to begin and end by exploring the life and claims of Jesus.

A Hard Truth

In a perfect world, every person who hears the truth about Jesus would believe and accept him as their Savior. Any honest look at the teachings of Scripture makes it impossible to do otherwise. But you and I live in a fallen world, not a perfect one, so not everyone is willing to listen.

My friends from the Atheist Club at Reading those many years ago found it impossible to argue with the evidence I presented them, yet still each of them chose to turn a deaf ear. After several hours of exploring the death, burial, and resurrection of Jesus, most of them were forced to admit that they had no other explanation than that he had physically risen from the grave. But it was a truth they were not yet ready to embrace. Atheism had become their religion, and it's hard to walk away from a religion that has come to define your life.

The good news is, that experience was more the exception than the rule. Most people I've shared with through the years are far more honest and open-minded. And when they hear the truth about Jesus, they are quick to embrace it. I have far more stories of joy and rejoicing than I do tales of rejection.

Once people hear and understand the story of Jesus, they almost always wonder why it took them so long to accept it.

It's All about Jesus

As believers, we are all expected to know how to defend our faith whenever it is questioned. The apostle Peter wrote, "Always be prepared to give an answer to everyone who asks you to give the reason for the hope that you have. But do this with gentleness and respect" (1 Pet. 3:15).

During my early years with Campus Crusade, I spent a great deal of time studying Christian apologetics, learning not just what I believed but why I believed it. I learned all I could about how to effectively talk about the validity of the New Testament documents. I read and studied numerous books from scholars in different parts of the world who had become followers of Jesus after studying the documentary evidence as agnostics. I spent so much time studying that I could soon hold my own in the most intense intellectual debate.

I'm glad I took the time to learn, because I want to be able to defend every aspect of my belief system when it comes under fire. But I've also learned what a distraction biblical debates can be. It's easy to get so caught up arguing about the times and dates of certain historical events or other semantics of Scripture that you never get around to discussing the most critical truth of the Christian faith: the person of Jesus!

Jesus is God's only Son, the redeemer of mankind. He's not a concept or an idea; he's the one and only Savior of the world. His life and teachings were never intended to be reduced to intellectual discourse or academic debate. And he doesn't need you and me to defend him. Jesus is fully capable of defending himself.

Today I'm convinced that the most effective way to share our faith with others is to talk about who Jesus is and what he has done in our lives. To tell our story and share what is in our hearts. To focus on the reality of Jesus in us, and what our relationship with him has done to transform the way we think and live.

Though I am a long way from being the man I desire to be, I've walked with Jesus for over forty-five years, and I know what it means to be his personal friend. I've experienced this relationship firsthand. Jesus is the first person I talk to when I wake up in the morning and the last person I talk to when I lie down at night. Since the day I accepted him into my life at the age of twenty-two, I've felt him daily guiding my steps and directing my days as we walk along the path of life together. I know his voice. I've felt his touch. I've experienced the joy of his presence. No one can tell me he's a myth, because I know him like I know my own brother.

That's what people long to hear. That's what the person of Jesus is all about. That's the message that breaks down walls and brings people into a real and personal relationship with Jesus.

There is supernatural power in the name of Jesus. That is perhaps the most important lesson you and I could possibly learn. And it's the one thing I try most to remember when I sit down and share my faith with someone.

When we talk about Jesus with others, he's not looking down from heaven, disengaged and disinterested. He is right there by our side, guiding our thoughts and directing our words. Whenever the name of Jesus is being discussed, he has a vested interest in the conversation. So you can be sure he's within arm's reach. You can likely hear his gentle voice if you listen.

Jesus is always there. Even when it feels like we are all alone.

Mercy in the Darkness

Years ago, just months after giving my life to Christ, while preparing to go to England with Campus Crusade, I went through a period of deep spiritual dryness and discouragement. It happened during my three-month training period at the University of California at Berkeley. For several weeks I couldn't seem to convince anyone to listen to me. It seemed that almost every person I tried to share with would either laugh in my face or be totally uninterested. I felt completely ineffective as a witness for Jesus.

One day my friend John sensed my frustration and sat with me on the steps of Sproul Hall in order to give me a few words of encouragement. It was a nice gesture, but nothing he said seemed to help. I can't remember the last time I had felt so beaten and depressed. I was someone who had always had a positive and sunny demeanor, so this was a new experience for me.

John placed his hand on my shoulder and prayed for me, then when he finished, he encouraged me to pray as well. I should have remained silent, but grief got the best of me.

I raised my eyes toward heaven, and in a moment of total despair and anguish I cried out to God, "I am so discouraged right now! No one I talk to is interested in hearing about you. I need a sign from you, Lord. I know you've called me to be your witness, and I need you to help me. I want the next person I meet to be ready to receive you as their Lord. If you can't do that, then you are not God!"

Even as the words left my lips, I regretted saying them. John quickly moved away so that the lightning bolt wouldn't strike us both. It was the most ignorant and arrogant prayer I had ever prayed. I would not ever recommend anyone else doing this, and I would never utter such a thing again. But it was an honest prayer from the depths of my spirit. I had never felt so lost and alone.

Thankfully, John was a true friend and stayed by my side, encouraging me in my darkest hour.

Just across the plaza in the student center was a lounge called the Bear's Lair, and I knew that it would be bustling with students at this time of the afternoon. Something in my spirit told me to go there, so I thanked John for listening and made my way down the steps of Sproul Hall. When I got to the Bear's Lair, the room was so crowded I could barely squeeze through the front door.

I stood at the entrance and scanned the large room. Every table and booth was occupied with three or four students. All except for one. In the middle of the room a young man sat by himself at a small booth, with an empty seat across from him. The minute I saw him, he looked in my direction and smiled. The two of us locked eyes, and he pointed to the empty seat, motioning for me to join him.

I looked over my shoulder to make sure I was the one he was looking at. It was such a strange occurrence. I couldn't remember anyone at Cal ever inviting me to join them at their table—especially a total stranger. I took a deep breath and made my way to his booth.

He introduced himself as Karl, and I thanked him for his kindness. Then in a slightly European accent he asked me, "So what are you doing here at Berkeley?"

I answered, "I'm here talking to students about how to have a personal relationship with Jesus if they are interested." Then in a moment of boldness, I leaned across the table and asked, "Are you interested?"

He smiled and said, "As a matter of fact, I am. I actually have a lot of questions about Jesus. I'd love to talk about him."

For the next hour, Karl and I sat and visited as I told him about Jesus. I began by sharing my personal journey, recapping the day I gave my heart to Jesus for the first time. Then I took out the *Four Spiritual Laws* booklet and asked if we could read through it together. We went over each point one by one. It had been a long time since I'd run across someone so interested in hearing the Good News of Jesus.

When we finished reading through the booklet, I asked if he'd like to invite Jesus into his life as his personal Lord and Savior, and he said yes. So right there in the middle of the noisy Bear's Lair, the two of us bowed our heads and prayed together as he dedicated his life to Jesus. When he finished praying, he raised his eyes to meet mine and his face was glowing. It was unlike anything I'd ever seen.

No Friend like Jesus

I've experienced the miraculous hand of God in a lot of different ways through the years, but nothing quite as profound or encouraging as my encounter with Karl those many years ago.

Even as I was sharing my faith with him, I knew in my heart that God had led me to his table. There was no doubt in my mind that the Holy Spirit had orchestrated our meeting.

I arranged to meet Karl two days later to follow up on our conversation, but he had somehow completely disappeared. He had told me he was on the track and field team, so when he didn't show up for our meeting, I stopped by the coach's office to ask about him. He said Karl was on the team, but no one had seen him for the past two days. So I went to the address he had given me. His housemother said that she, too, had not seen him for two days. It was as if he had never existed. One day he was at school, and the next he had vanished. No one at Berkeley ever saw him again. And no one was able to explain his disappearance.

To this day, I'm convinced that God sent an angel to encourage me in my hour of need. At the darkest moment of my life, he found a way to comfort me.

That's the kind of good and loving God we serve. No matter how long I live, no matter how dark things seem or how hopeless they feel, no matter where the road of life takes me, I will never have a friend like Jesus.

And neither will you.

As long as I have strength in my bones and breath in my lungs, I'll spend my days talking to people about my friend Jesus. Every person deserves to hear about the most life-changing relationship in the universe, and I won't stop until he takes me home to spend eternity with him in heaven.

The apostle Paul wrote, "For what I received I passed on to you as of first importance: that Christ died for our sins according to the Scriptures, that he was buried, that he was raised on the third day according to the Scriptures" (1 Cor. 15:3–4).

Is there a message on earth that brings more weight and urgency?

You and I both know the answer. And I think our friends deserve to know it as well.

Jesus is everything, and all of life revolves around the person of Jesus. And you and I are called to have a deep and personal relationship with him—not only during our days on earth but for all eternity in heaven.

That, my friends, is very, *very* good news!

Afterword

Since this is an afterword, you may have just finished reading Jim's book. Or you may have turned here first. If so, I enthusiastically encourage you to go back and read the book. I guarantee *The Power of One-on-One* is worth it!

Jim Stump is the real deal. I love who he is and what he does. Jim's brother John is a friend, and John's son Dan, Jim's nephew, married my daughter Angela. I couldn't be happier to have grandsons with the last name Stump. Jim and I don't exchange Christmas gifts (you first, Jim), but I hear great reports about him at family gatherings.

Years ago, when I first spent time with Jim, I was struck with his genuineness. He's all about Jesus and the power of the Holy Spirit, who alone can draw hearts to God.

I've read books about evangelism that credit a technique. Jim credits the gospel and the power of God. It's a relief to know the work of salvation can't be done by us. We're "just" the messengers . . . but what a job!

I appreciate how Jim models loving people and investing in them. He doesn't want them just to go through the motions, but to follow Christ with abandonment for a lifetime. And he's there to help them do just that.

When it comes to sharing the gospel, Jim seems to be a natural. But this kind of "natural" is not like a fish swimming. It's like a veteran tennis player swinging a racquet. A fish may be born swimming, but a tennis player wasn't born holding a racquet. He was coached and corrected, and he worked hard to achieve that "natural" swing. I was encouraged to learn it was once difficult for Jim to share his faith!

I coached high school tennis for ten years. Coaches tell players to do seemingly unnatural things. Some players quickly conclude, "This doesn't work," and go back to their old habits. But unless they're willing to work on the skills coaches offer, they won't be great tennis players. It's those willing to learn who receive huge payoffs.

Raised in an unbelieving home, I vividly remember coming to Christ as a teenager. I've had many experiences of sharing Jesus with people at schools, on planes, and on tennis courts. Some friends think I'm a natural-born evangelist. But I'm not! I find the hardest thing is choosing to open my mouth. Once I do, the Lord graciously gives me the words. Sharing my faith isn't as "natural" for me as for Jim Stump, but it's far more natural than it once was. For that I thank God.

I found *The Power of One-on-One* to be clear, direct, and refreshing. Reading it made me eager to be more intentional about sharing my faith and mentoring others.

As we walk away from this book, let's not put it behind us but in front of us. Everyone we meet has exactly the same need—to know and follow Jesus Christ. He did the hard work of redemption. He calls us to do our part, one-on-one, sharing the Good News with those who desperately need him and helping them grow.

Thanks, Jim, for inspiring and coaching us to do exactly that!

Randy Alcorn
Author of *Heaven*, *Safely Home*, and *Eternity*

Notes

1. Harold Ockenga, Robert Lamont, and Carl Henry, "The Evangelical World Prospect," *Christianity Today*, October 28, 2008, http://www.christianitytoday.com/ct/2008/octoberweb-only/144-26.0.html?start=4.

2. The Quotable Christian, "Salvation," 2004, http://www.pietyhilldesign.com/gcq/quotepages/salvation.html.

3. Previously published as Bill Bright, *Have You Heard of the Four Spiritual Laws?* (Wayne, NJ: New Life Publications, 1993).

4. For those interested, I recommend a classic book titled *How to Win Friends and Influence People* by Dale Carnegie. Though it was written many years ago, the principles it espouses are timeless and helpful when it comes to relating and sharing your faith with others.

5. Dr. Bill Bright, *Would You Like to Know God Personally?* (Wayne, NJ: New Life Publications, 1998).

6. Brennan Manning, *The Ragamuffin Gospel: Embracing the Unconditional Love of God* (Sisters, OR: Multnomah Books, 1990), 29.

Jim Stump is the founder of Sports Challenge and has been a one-on-one mentor to many hundreds of Stanford student athletes for over forty years. He has also served as chaplain for the San Francisco 49ers and the San Francisco Giants. A graduate of Wheaton College, Stump lives in California with his wife, Linda. To learn more about Jim's ministry, visit his website, www.sportschallenge.org.

Frank Martin is the author or coauthor of twenty books. A frequent collaborator, he has written books with such notable personalities as Nicky Cruz, Jerry Jenkins, Tim LaHaye, Dr. O. S. Hawkins, Wally Armstrong, and Jimmy Evans. He lives in Colorado with his wife, Ruthie, and their two children. For more information, please visit www.frankmartin.net.

Sports Challenge

A ministry devoted to the support, encouragement, and faith-building of Stanford student athletes.

If you have been encouraged, blessed, and challenged by reading *The Power of One-on-One,* and you want to learn more about how you can pray and impact people for the kingdom, visit **www.sportschallenge.org.**